Famous Phrases from History

by
Charles F. Hemphill, Jr.

Jefferson & London : McFarland
1982

Dedicated to my grandchildren,
with hope that some ideas
from the past may be useful in
our future.

Library of Congress Cataloging in Publication Data

Hemphill, Charles F.
   Famous phrases from history.

   Includes index.
   1. Quotations, English. 2. History—Miscellanea.
I. Title.
PN6083.H38   082   82-7217
ISBN 0-89950-052-8 (pbk.) AACR2

Copyright © 1982 by Charles F. Hemphill

Manufactured in the United States of America

McFarland & Company, Inc., Publishers,
   Box 611, Jefferson, North Carolina 28640

Table of Contents

Introduction

This is a collection of famous phrases from history, both spoken and written.

Perhaps all thinking people have associated themselves in imagination with the powerful figures and moving forces of history. Some utterances in every age have transcended time and national boundaries. Passing into the language, these phrases have crystallized great issues of the past for the understanding of future generations.

Many of these phrases originated spontaneously under the stress of dramatic, tension-filled confrontations, with the future of individuals or even entire nations hanging in the balance. Some originated with extraordinary men or women who were intent on motivating others to build a more civilized world. A few of these phrases were not uttered in response to a specific situation, but as a general truth. Some can be credited only to tradition, but the facts surrounding the tradition are so compelling that the phrase cannot be ignored.

Leaders are often known only by their acts. But sometimes their words alone have echoed down the years, immortalizing both the speaker and the occasion.

In a sense, these are phrases of significance to every age — words that fill life with the sunlight and shadows that illuminate and darken the swift voyage of humankind.

Phrases included are divided into three categories: those from American history, those from British, French, and other European and World history, and those from ancient (or "classical") times.

Phrases from
American History

"So they committed themselves to the will of God and resolved to proseede."

(William Bradford, 1620)

William Bradford (1589-1657) joined the Pilgrims after religious persecution and came to the New World on the *Mayflower*. On the death of the first governor of the new colony, Bradford was elected governor. With the exception of a few years when he refused to serve, Bradford remained as the Pilgrim's leader until his death in 1657.

Some of the Pilgrims set sail from Southampton, England, in August, 1620, in the *Mayflower*, while others in the company set out in the *Speedwell*. After a short time, however, it was apparent that the *Speedwell* was too leaky to proceed. The two vessels then turned back and all of the pilgrims destined for the New World crowded on-to the *Mayflower*.

Bradford's account of the Pilgrims in his "Of Plymouth Plantation," "Bradford's History of the Plymouth Settlement," and other writings (actually, diary entries) furnished clear insight into the Pilgrims' problems and their bravery. As Bradford told it, "So they committed themselves to the will of God and resolved to proseede," in spite of one ship that was unseaworthy and another that was almost.

"Who would have thought it?"

(General Edward Braddock, 1755)

The French and Indian War was in full swing in 1755, with the British and her American Colonies pitted against the French and Indian allies.

British General Edward Braddock marched on the French fort, Ft. Duquesne, located near present day Pittsburgh, Pennsylvania, at the head of 2200 troops. Included in Braddock's forces were 800 Colonial troops from Virginia and New York. The Virginia contingent was headed by young George Washington.

Braddock already had a considerable reputation from service in the English army on European battlefields. Benjamin Franklin, an old friend, tried to warn Braddock of Indian ambush. Young Washington also tried to explain to Braddock that the Indians used different tactics from those of European armies, but Braddock would not listen. Instead, the confident English General said that the French and Indians would neither fight from ambush nor give open opposition when they saw his well-trained redcoats.

While Braddock's troops passed through a deep ravine just beyond the Monongahela River, they were ambushed by 70 French regulars, 150 Canadians, and 650 Indian allies. Some of the Indians did not have guns, but all the attackers were hidden behind trees, undergrowth, and rocky outcroppings. Splendid soldiers in the open battlefields of Europe, the British regulars were bewildered by the deadly fire. The redcoats huddled together in confusion as the withering fire continued. After a time they "ran as sheep pursued by dogs," George Washington later wrote his mother.

A brave soldier, if not an especially astute general, Braddock tried to disperse his troops to places of safety and to halt their mad flight. In leading the Virginians, Washington had two horses shot from under him. Braddock was wounded in the lung.

Still able to command for a time, Braddock was carried from the field in a cart. By the time some order had been restored, the French and Indians had vanished into the wilderness. In shock from his wound and in amazement at the "hit and run" tactics of frontier fighting, Braddock repeated over and over, "Who would have thought it!" Later he told his aides, "We shall know better how to deal with them another time." Four days after the battle, General Braddock died.

He was buried in two blankets and all the carts and wagons in his supply train drove over his grave. The Indians would have taken up Braddock's body and scalped the general had they known he lay concealed under the ruts cut by his wagons.

"Taxation without representation is tyranny!"

(James Otis, 1768)

James Otis (1725-1783) was an American patriot who was bitterly opposed to the British King's imposition of special taxes for the Colonies. When George III imposed the so-called Stamp Act, Colonial opposition to this measure became intense. This act required the Colonists to purchase a tax stamp for every newspaper, pamphlet, deed, legal paper, or license they acquired — even for a college diploma.

Much of the Colonists' objections came into being after their leaders repeated Otis' famous statement, "Taxation without representation is tyranny."

Physically assaulted by the King's tax collectors because of his criticism of their methods, Otis received a head wound which, some historians feel, caused him to lose his reason.

"Millions yet unborn may be the miserable sharers in the event."

(Samuel Adams, 1771)

Perhaps it was Samuel Adams (1722-1803) who did as much as any other single individual to bring about the American Revolution.

Relatively unknown on the national scene in 1763, Adams quickly came to public attention through his literary and oratorical skill. About this time, George III's ministers were endeavoring to control and regulate all American shipping and trade, to make royal officials independent of Colonial legislatures, to garrison the Colonies with troops in the settler's homes, and to raise direct revenue by taxes on imports to America.

All of these measures Adams opposed loudly. Adams also took the lead in planning the "Boston Massacre," which was actually only a fight in which soldiers killed Colonial citizens. The overreaction by the British troops led to the withdrawal of soldiers for a time, but they were then returned by King George.

During 1771 and 1772 the strong voice of Adams seemed to be alone in reminding his countrymen that the basic intentions of the British had not been altered. "Let us remember that if we suffer tamely a lawless attack upon our liberty," said Adams, "that millions yet unborn may be the miserable sharers in the event."

Continuing to speak out, Adams was one of the Signers of the Declaration of Independence. After the Revolution he became governor of Massachusetts.

"There never was a good war or a bad peace."

(Benjamin Franklin, 1773)

The leaders of the American Revolution were not seeking to stir up war, but to "win their rights as free Englishmen" from the King who discriminated against them, George III.

In a letter to another Colonial leader, Josiah Quincy, Benjamin Franklin wrote on September 11, 1773, "There never was a good war or a bad peace."

"I have but one lamp by which my feet are guided."

(Patrick Henry, 1774)

Perhaps few men have ever been more eloquent than Patrick Henry (1736-1799), the backwoods Virginia lawyer. Speaking before the First Continental Congress, October 14, 1774, of the Colonials' quarrel with the British King, George III, Henry said:

"It is natural for man to indulge in the illusions of hope. We are apt to shut our eyes against a painful truth.... Is this the part of wise men, engaged in a great and arduous struggle for liberty? Are we disposed to be the number of those who, having eyes, see not, and having ears, hear not....

I have but one lamp by which my feet are guided, and that is the lamp of experience....

If we wish to be free; if we mean to preserve inviolate those inestimable privileges for which we have been so long contending ... we must fight.

The battle, sir, is not to the strong alone; it is to the vigilant, the active, the brave...."

"Give me liberty, or give me death!"

(Patrick Henry, 1775)

Patrick Henry, through his intrepidity and his oratory, became one of the leading voices that launched the American Revolution.

While Thomas Jefferson was still a college student, he recorded Henry's ringing words in May, 1765, at the time George III imposed the Stamp Act on the American Colonies. Henry told the Virginia Legislature: "Caesar had his Brutus; Charles the First, his Cromwell; and George the Third"—("Treason!" shouted the Speaker; "Treason! Treason!" echoed others) ... and George the Third may profit by their example," continued Henry. "If this be treason, make the most of it!"

Later, while representing Virginia at the first Colonial Congress at Philadelphia in 1774, Henry told the assembly, "The distinctions between Virginians, Pennsylvanians, New Yorkers, and New Englanders are no more. I am not a Virginian, but an American!"

On March 23, 1775, Henry thought that the time had come for the Colonies to arm themselves, and he so stated to the Second Virginia Convention, in Richmond. Some of the other delegates were electrified, but Henry continued, "Gentlemen may cry peace! peace!—but there is no peace! The war is actually begun! The next gale that sweeps from the North will bring to our ears the crash of resounding arms! Our brethren are already in the field! ... Is life so dear, or peace so sweet, as to be purchased at the price of chains and slavery? Forbid it. Almighty God! I know not what course others may take; but as for me, give me liberty, or give me death!"

"One if by land, and two if by sea."

(traditional signal, Paul Revere's "ride," 1775)

Paul Revere (1735-1818), a Boston silversmith, was one of the leaders in the American Revolutionary War.

Realizing that they might be pushed to actual war with George III's Great Britain, the Colonists had been assembling supplies and munitions at Concord, about 20 miles from Boston. General Thomas Gage, British commander, sent out 800 troops to destroy or seize the Colonials' supplies and also to arrest Samuel Adams, John Hancock, and other revolutionary leaders.

Working with another patriot (Colonel Conant of the Charlestown Committee of Safety), Paul Revere had arranged to receive a signal so that other patriots could be warned. One lantern was to be hung in the Old North Church steeple if the British were coming by land and two lanterns if they were arriving by ship. Actually, Revere made two "midnight rides," often dated as on April 16, 1775, one to warn of the need for protection of patriot supplies, and the other to warn of the possible arrest of patriot leaders. Because of Revere's warnings, the patriots were able to assemble militia to defend their military supplies at Concord and at Bunker Hill. In addition, revolutionary leaders managed to evade arrest. Revere himself fell into British hands, but was released after a day.

"If they want to have a war,
let it begin here!"

(Captain John Parker, 1775)

On April 19, 1775 General Gage's British troops were seeking to find and destroy supplies and arms that were being collected by American patriots. Gage's troops encountered a group of 50 or 60 near Lexington, where some of the arms and supplies were supposedly stored. The British ordered the militiamen to disperse, and almost immediately fired into their ranks. Eight of the patriots were killed and the Redcoats themselves suffered some casualties in the resulting exchange of fire. All in all, the affair at Lexington was little more than a skirmish, but it put the Colonies on notice that actual fighting had begun. As John Parker, the Colonial militia commander, said "If they want to have a war, let it begin here!"

"In the name of the great Jehovah and the Continental Congress."

(Ethan Allen, 1775)

Ethan Allen (1737-1789) was the daring commander of Colonial soldiers in the Revolutionary War. From the New Hampshire area, Allen's troops were called the "Green Mountain Boys."

In the early hours of the morning of May 10, 1775, Allen's Colonials surprised the British troops at Fort Ticonderoga. Some of the Green Mountain Boys climbed the walls of the fort without being observed by the sentry. Once inside, Allen's soldiers managed to open the gates to the rest of the defenders. The fort fell with hardly a fight. The British commander, Captain LaPlace, surrendered with his breeches in his hands. Allen ordered surrender "In the name of the great Jehovah and the Continental Congress."

"Don't fire until you see the whites of their eyes!"

(attributed to Israel Putnam, 1775)

Israel Putnam (1718-1790) was an American soldier who fought for the British and American side in the French and Indian wars. Sent out in 1758 on an individual expedition to capture stores from the enemy, Putnam was captured and tortured until close to death by the Indians. Eventually rescued by a French officer, Putnam was exchanged for other prisoners.

Later, when the Revolutionary War began, Putnam became a brigadier general in a regiment of Connecticut rebels. According to the story, Putnam was plowing his farm when he heard that fighting might begin at Bunker Hill. Hurrying to the scene, "old Put," as he was called, steadied the inexperienced Colonials. Afraid that his men would fire before the British Redcoats got into good range, Putnam reportedly ordered, "Don't fire until you see the whites of their eyes."

"Stand! Stand! The ground's your own...!"

(Joseph Warren, 1775)

Joseph Warren, a 34-year old Massachusetts doctor, was a major figure in events leading to the outbreak of the Revolutionary War. In April, 1775, he was elected president of the Provisional Congress, and he was a major general in the Massachusetts militia.

As a volunteer, Warren joined the Colonial forces that had assembled on Breed's Hill and nearby Bunker Hill. When the Redcoats ("Lobsterbacks") charged, uncertain what to do, the patriots wavered. "Stand! Stand! The ground's your own, my braves!" shouted Warren. Encouraged, the Colonials returned the fire, causing numerous losses to the British regulars, but Warren fell to a bullet in the head.

Bunker Hill was not a great battle from the standpoint of soldiers involved. But it showed the Colonials that raw, untrained patriots could perform with great credit when they believed in their cause. According to Daniel Webster, Warren was "the first great martyr" of the American Revolution.

"If particular care and attention are not paid to the ladies, we ... will not hold ourselves bound to obey any laws in which we have no voice or representation."

(Abigail Adams, 1775)

Throughout his life John Adams (1735-1826) was away from home for extended periods, as politician, congressman, ambassador, senator, and second President of the United States. The many letters sent Adams by his wife, Abigail (1744-1818), have thus furnished modern scholars considerable insight into the social and political conditions of that day, though, like other women in colonial times, Mrs. Adams took little part in public life.

She did not mince words in pointing out inequalities, however. In 1775, writing to her husband at the Continental Congress in Philadelphia, Abigail said:

"I desire you would remember the ladies.... Do not put such unlimited power into the hands of husbands. Remember all men would be tyrants if they could. If particular care and attention are not paid to the ladies, we are determined to foment a rebellion and will not hold ourselves bound to obey any laws in which we have no voice or representation."

"resolved to die free men, rather than to live as slaves"

(Resolution, Second Continental Congress, 1775)

In June, 1775 the Second Continental Congress passed "a Declaration on the Causes and Necessity of Taking Up Arms," a statement that led to the American Revolution. Feeling that liberty had to be won at the risk of their lives, members of the Continental Congress "...resolved to die free men, rather than to live as slaves." Much later, in World War II, President Franklin D. Roosevelt repeated this phrase coined by these earlier patriots, describing our stand against the Nazis and Japanese.

"Don't tread on me!"

(motto on U.S.S. *Alfred,* 1775)

"Don't tread on me!" was a motto used on the first official American flag. It was flown by Lt. John Paul Jones on Commodore Esek Hopkin's flagship *Alfred,* in the Colonial navy.

"There must always be one tax to keep up the right."

(George III, 1775)

Many of the American Colonists thought of themselves as free

Englishmen, who had come to the New World at great sacrifice. They believed that they had the same rights as other Englishmen in Great Britain. But the King, George III, thought they should pay taxes that were not levied in England because it was expensive to protect the crown's far-flung Colonies. Apparently it never got through to the King that British trading companies made a great profit from the Colonies.

For their part, the Colonies protested bitterly that they were taxed without any opportunity to vote on the taxes in question. When the King's taxes were repealed, the opposition in the Colonies subsided. But George III stubbornly insisted that not all taxes on the Colonies could be abolished, saying in 1775, "There must always be one tax to keep up the right" (i.e., any sort of tax just to prove that taxation itself was lawful).

"We must all hang together, or assuredly we shall all hang separately!"

(Benjamin Franklin, 1776)

By the summer of 1776 the American Colonists' war with Britain had already begun. Battles had been fought with the Redcoats at Lexington, Concord, and at Breed's Hill. George Washington had been named to head the Colonial army. Many patriots were echoing the sentiments of Samuel Adams, "Is not America already independent? Why not then declare it!"

On June 7, 1776, Richard Henry Lee of Virginia moved in the Continental Congress for a declaration of independence. After a committee was set up, Thomas Jefferson spent 18 days writing and polishing the draft, and the final version was adopted on July 4th.

It was a time of great peril for the outspoken patriots, since the British army was one of the strongest in the world. Signing such a declaration could be equivalent to placing one's own signature on a death warrant for treason. The Colonists could only hope that their divided, inexperienced peoples could unite to defeat King George's seasoned troops. Perhaps a few who signed the historic document fixed their signatures in response to the rash of patriotic fever that swept the Colonies. There is good evidence, however, to believe the majority of the Signers had carefully looked at the consequences of failure and had made an unflinching decision for independence.

Benjamin Franklin, at 70 too old to fight in the Colonial army, spoke for the Signers on that historic day: he told them, "We must all hang together, or assuredly we shall all hang separately."

"All men are created equal."

(Thomas Jefferson, 1776)

No document in American history ever meant more to the people than the Declaration of Independence. Written by Thomas Jefferson (1743-1846) in a Philadelphia boarding house, it was also of great importance in the cause of liberty throughout the entire world.

In 1776, people in Europe would have regarded anyone as mad who declared that "All men are created equal." The social and financial positions of the Europeans were such that individuals seldom rose above the station of their birth.

"When in the course of human events, it becomes necessary for one people to dissolve the political bands which have connected them with another..."

(Declaration of Independence, 1776)

Hoping to win concessions from Britain, the Second Continental Congress disclaimed any intent of revolting against the crown. But about the time of the Congress, Thomas Paine's pamphlet *Common Sense* was widely circulated among the American Colonies. Paine's writings urged independence for America by revolting against the king.

Paine's views gained wide support among the people. On May 15, 1775, Virginia instructed her delegates to the Second Continental Congress to move for a declaration of independence. This action quickly gathered momentum, as other Colonies followed. A committee of five men was designated by the Congress to work out a proposed draft. The five appointed were John Adams, Thomas Jefferson, Benjamin Franklin, Roger Sherman, and Robert R. Livingston.

Jefferson, familiar with the writings of John Locke, the English political theorist and philosopher, set himself to the job of polishing the committee's proposal. The result that followed was one of the most powerful political documents ever written.

"I only regret that I have but one life to lose for my country."

(Nathan Hale, 1776)

Under the pressure of defeat by the British at the Battle of Long Island, General George Washington pulled back his discouraged troops to Manhattan Island. Then Washington asked his experienced officers to recommend trusted young men to act as spies to determine from which direction the powerful British fleet and army of General Howe would next strike.

Lt. Col. Thomas Knowlton suggested Nathan Hale, a 21-year-old former school teacher who had previously effected the capture of a British supply sloop from under the very guns of the man-of-war *Asia*. Hale accepted the assignment and assumed his old dress as a schoolmaster, complete with his Yale diploma.

With damning evidence still on his person, Hale was captured by British troops in New York while making his way north toward Washington's lines on September 21, 1776. The British commander offered Hale the rank of captain and a sum of money if he would change his allegiance, but Hale was too honorable even to pretend to accept a offer.

Without the formality of a military trial, General Howe condemned Hale to death on the following day. Hale's jailor, Provost Marshal William Cunningham, refused him a Bible, chaplain, or paper to write letters.

Immediately before his death on September 22, 1776, Hale uttered the immortal words for which he will always be remembered, "I only regret that I have but one life to lose for my country."

"These are the times that try men's souls."

(Thomas Paine, 1776)

An English idealist, Thomas Paine was hounded out of his native country when he campaigned bitterly for individual rights.

In October, 1774, Paine arrived in America carrying letters of recommendation from Benjamin Franklin, who was then living in London. By January, 1776, Paine had become one of the most powerful writers in the cause of American freedom. For several years sentiment had been building among the Colonists for Paine's summons to liberty, expressed in his pamphlets: *Common Sense* and *The American Crisis.*

In the latter, dated December 19, 1776, Paine wrote: "Society in every state is a blessing, but government, even in its best state is but a necessary evil; in its worst state an intolerable one.... [T]he palaces of kings are built upon the ruins ... of paradise."

Later, when it seemed the Revolutionary cause might be lost, Paine inspired many who were wavering: "These are the times that try men's souls. The summer soldier and the sunshine patriot will, in this crisis, shrink from the service of their country; but he that stands it now deserves the love and thanks of man and woman.... [T]yranny, like hell, is not easily conquered!"

Paine's words were eagerly read by the Colonials. One patriot said his "words were written in the blood which stained the snow at Valley Forge." General Washington wrote that *"The American Crisis* worked a change on the minds of many men."

*"The tree of liberty must be refreshed
from time to time with the blood of patriots."*

(Thomas Jefferson, 1787)

Eleven years after he signed the Declaration of Independence, Benjamin Rush made an "Address to the people of the United States." In this speech, Rush said, "The American war is over, but this is far from being the case of the American revolution. On the contrary, nothing but the first act of the great drama is closed."

After the establishment of the United States government, many of the young nation's leaders voiced the belief that a nation of free people could never rest on past accomplishments—that the enjoyment of freedom demanded a continuing price. Franklin, Washington, and Jefferson all expressed such convictions.

Jefferson said that freedom cannot long be taken for granted. "The tree of liberty must be refreshed from time to time with the blood of patriots."

The statements made by Rush and Jefferson may well be as valid today as at the time the statements were made. The history of the world shows that after one tyranny has been put down, another has often made an appearance. If people are going to expect freedom as their right, then there may come a time when they must be willing to defend it.

*"We beat them today,
or Mollie Stark's a widow!"*

(John Stark, 1777)

A native of Londonderry, New Hampshire, John Stark (1728-1822), had been captured by the Indians. He lived in captivity for some time before escaping. Later, he fought as a captain with Robert Rogers' Rangers during the French and Indian Wars. When the American Revolution broke out, he was appointed a colonel, after serving at Bunker Hill.

As commander of the New Hampshire troops at the Battle of Bennington, he led the attack on the British with the command, "There they are boys. We beat them today or Mollie Stark's a widow!"

Stark's troops were victorious, leading the way to British General Burgoyne's surrender at Saratoga.

"Here comes Molly Pitcher!"

(Revolutionary cry, 1778)

Few of the men in General George Washington's army had any training as professional soldiers, but most of them could handle a rifle and shoot well. However, the Colonials were sadly lacking in personnel with experience in supply or the handling of commissary duties.

Like many other Colonial soldiers' wives, Mary Ludwig Hays, nicknamed "Molly," joined her young husband in camp and made herself useful by cooking, washing, and performing supply duties. Her young husband, John Casper Hays, had enlisted as a gunner in the First Pennsylvania Artillery, and together they spent the winters of 1777 and 1778 with Washington at Valley Forge.

On June 28, 1778, Mary Hays followed close behind as her husband's company went into action against the British at the Battle of Monmouth. This occurred on one of the hottest days of an unusually hot summer, and the heat and the strenuous action made the soldiers extremely thirsty. Observing their condition, Mrs. Hays filled a pitcher at a nearby spring, and ran from soldier to soldier carrying water to the troops. Unable to remember her name, grateful troops shouted, "Here comes Molly Pitcher!"

After a time Mary's husband was wounded while firing his cannon. Observing how his absence handicapped the gun crew, Mary immediately took her husband's place and helped to keep the gun in action. After the battle, "Molly Pitcher," as she was then called, took her wounded husband to their home at Carlisle, Pennsylvania, to recuperate.

In her declining years the Pennsylvania legislature voted this female hero a pension of $40 a year for life, a sum that would buy far more in those days than at the present.

"I have not yet begun to fight!"

(John Paul Jones, 1779)

Captain John Paul Jones has sometimes been called the "Father of the United States Navy." In 1775 he became first lieutenant of the *Alfred,* the first naval ship bought by the Continental Congress. Later he became captain of the *Ranger.* Taking the Revolutionary War to the British, Jones raided English shipping in the Irish Sea in 1778. He captured the British sloop *Drake,* and took seven merchantmen to France as prizes of war.

On a subsequent voyage, Jones sailed the *Bonhomme Richard* into the Irish Sea. There, on September 23, 1779, Jones' ship attacked the *Serapis,* a larger and better equipped British man-of-war. With their ships so close that their rigging was entangled, the British commander called on Jones to surrender. But the American commander called out, "I have not yet begun to fight!" After three more hours of hand-to-hand struggle, the British finally surrendered. The *Bonhomme Richard* was so badly damaged that it sank the next day, but Jones sailed away to France in the *Serapis.*

"To be prepared for war is one of the most effectual means of preserving peace."

(President George Washington, 1790)

Spoken on January 8, 1790, in his first address to Congress, by the first President of the United States, George Washington (1732-1799).

"Steer clear of permanent alliances..."

(George Washington, 1796)

George Washington always urged his countrymen to stay away from habitual alliances with others. In his September 17, 1796, Farewell Address upon leaving public life (which was never delivered orally but through the press) he said:
"It is our true foreign policy to steer clear of permanent alliances with any portion of the foreign world, so far, I mean, as we are now at liberty to do it."

"Millions for defense — not one cent for tribute!"

(Robert Goodloe Harper, 1796)

Charles Coatesworth Pinckney (1746-1825), to whom this quotation is generally, and erroneously attributed, was a soldier under General George Washington, who was himself eventually promoted to general. After the war he was a member of the Constitutional Convention in Philadelphia.

A frequent military rival of the British during this period of history, France had sent considerable aid to the Colonists during the American Revolution. By 1796 the new American nation was at peace with England. Resuming one of her military disputes with the British, France demanded that the United States again declare war with England. Having no real cause for war at the time, the United States Government sent Pinckney and other diplomats to France, to negotiate with the French Minister Talleyrand. The United States, being still a young and weak nation, wanted to remain at peace with both France and England.

Taylleyrand and his ministers made numerous demands on the Americans. At one time Talleyrand's representatives demanded that the United States pay tribute to France to keep from becoming further involved. To this, Pinckney indignantly replied, "No! No! Not a sixpence!"

After Pinckney returned to the United States he was toasted at a dinner honoring John Marshall. The toast, by Robert Goodloe Harper, was: "Millions for defense — not one cent for tribute!"

"First in war, first in peace,
and first in the hearts of his countrymen."

(Henry Lee, 1799)

When George Washington died in 1799, Henry Lee of Virginia (1756-1818) presented a resolution in December to the United States House of Representatives to honor the first President. Lee said that Washington was "first" in all these ways.

"This little rivulet yields
its distant tribute to the parent ocean."

(Meriwether Lewis, 1805)

Captain Meriwether Lewis (1774-1809) was the leader of the Lewis and Clark Expedition. Lewis' party was sent by President Thomas Jefferson to explore the vast, unknown territory that the United States bought from France in 1803 (the "Louisiana Purchase"). The expedition was made up of 31 men, including 26 army men and two Indian interpreters.

The purpose of the expedition was to learn something about what the region was like, and to examine its resources and inhabitants.

With a scientific background, Lewis kept a diary with entries about plants, animals, mineral resources, geographic features, and the Indians along the way. In August, 1805, Lewis realized that he had crossed over the continental divide, and that even the tiny streams flowed toward the Pacific, rather than the Atlantic. At one such trickle Lewis stopped and noted in his diary, "This little rivulet yields its distant tribute to the parent ocean."

Spending the winter of 1805-1806 on the Pacific coast near present-day Astoria, Oregon, a diary account said that the party lacked "every necessity but the gallant spirit with which each member of the party was plentifully endowed." The trip was a 9,000 mile journey that took about two and a half years.

"By heaven that ship is ours!"

(Captain Isaac Hull, 1812)

During the war of 1812 the fledgling American navy came face to face with the British navy, at that time the strongest sea power in the world for over 200 years.

Captain of the American warship *Constitution* (44 guns), Isaac Hull (1773-1843) was surrounded by the *Africa* (64 guns), *Belvedira* (36 guns), *Guerrière* (38 guns), *Shannon* (38 guns) and the *Aeolus* (32 guns). Hull managed to outsail all the British ships, however, and to escape. A few weeks later, on August 19, 1812, the *Constitution* met the *Guerrière* alone and quickly sank it, after Hull's famous cry, "By heaven that ship is ours!"

Because of the ability of the *Constitution* to take enemy cannon balls, the ship was popularly called "Old Ironsides." From having no navy worth mentioning, the United States had come to be a power with a feeling of confident hope.

"Don't give up the ship!"

(Captain James Lawrence, 1813)

James Lawrence (1781-1813) had joined the fledgling United States navy as a midshipman in 1798. Later he distinguished himself in the war with the Tripoli pirates in 1804 and 1805.

In the war between the United States and England in 1812, Lawrence was given command of the *Chesapeake*. With a young and poorly-trained crew, Lawrence had little time to prepare for battle before the Chesapeake met the British ship *Shannon*. On June 1, 1813, the two vessels closed to a distance of "half a pistol shot," and Lawrence was badly wounded in the fight.

Seeing that the battle was going poorly for the Americans, Lawrence refused to be carried below decks, so he could continue to command. Lawrence's historic order, "Don't give up the ship!" became a watchword of the new nation's Navy.

In spite of the Captain's entreaties, however, the *Chesapeake* was overrun and captured by the powerful crew of the *Shannon*. The *Chesapeake* was then taken to Halifax, Nova Scotia, where Lawrence died of his wounds.

"We have met the enemy and they are ours!"

(Oliver Hazard Perry, 1813)

Oliver Hazard Perry (1785-1819) had no naval command when the War of 1812 broke out, but he was soon placed in charge of the small fleet on Lake Erie. On his flagship the *Lawrence,* Perry flew a flag with the motto "Don't Give Up the Ship," the words of American Captain James Lawrence, who had died a short time earlier.

In Perry's first engagement with the British, the *Lawrence* was outgunned and sunk by the British. Perry then went by rowboat to another of his ships, the *Niagara,* which he brought into close action. Two British ships bore down on the *Niagara,* but the British vessels became entangled. The *Niagara* then raked them with cannon shot until they surrendered. Soon after, the entire fleet of six British ships surrendered. As a naval battle, this was not one of major proportions. But the British surrender gave the United States undisputed control of the entire Great Lakes area.

Perry's message to his headquarters read, "We have met the enemy and they are ours!"

Subsequently Perry died of yellow fever while on a diplomatic mission to South America for the United States State Department.

"Boys, elevate them guns a little lower!"

(General Andrew Jackson, 1815)

On January 8, 1815, Andrew Jackson's motley, ill-trained army of 6,000 sailors, city Creoles, Santo Domingans, Baratarian pirates, and a few regulars, decisively defeated 8,000 British veterans at the Battle of New Orleans.

The War of 1812 had already ended when the battle was fought, but communications from Europe were so slow that the antagonists were not made aware for some time after the battle.

Lord Packenham, the British commander, began his attack too late, as he waited until after daybreak for the fog to dissipate, and he marched his troops in orderly rows against the American defenses. Jackson had managed to obtain bales of cotton and other breatworks, behind which his position was almost impregnable. Packenham suffered 2,000 casualties, while Jackson's losses were only 13 killed and 58 wounded.

The American artillery proved particularly effective during the battle, after following Jackson's homespun order.

"Our country, may she always be in the right; but our country, right or wrong!"

(Stephen Decatur, 1816)

Stephen Decatur (1779-1820) was one of the most daring and successful officers in the United States Navy during its early history. He was acknowledged to have been a hero both in the war with Tripoli (1804-1805) and in the War of 1812 when he fought the British.

In a banquet at Norfolk, Virginia, in 1816, Decatur gave a toast: "Our country, may she always be in the right, but our country, right or wrong." (Slightly different versions of this phrase are sometimes given.)

Decatur made an enemy of a digraced officer who thought that Decatur and other officers were persecuting him. According to a custom of the time, this officer (James Barron) challenged Decatur to a duel. Decatur died in 1820 as a result of a wound sustained in this duel, at Bladensburg, Maryland.

"The American Continents ... are henceforth not to be considered as subjects for future colonization by any European powers."

(President James Monroe, 1823)

This statement was a portion of the famous Monroe Doctrine, in which the American President warned European powers they could no longer make colonial claims to territory in the New World.

In the summer of 1823 word had reached Washington that several European nations would hold a congress to settle colonial disputes in the Americas — to divide areas of influence.

Acting on his own initiative, James Monroe (1758-1851) drafted the statement that "The American Continents ... are henceforth not to be considered as subjects for future colonization by any European powers." Monroe added that any intervention would be regarded as the "manifestation of an unfriendly disposition toward the United States." He delivered the text of his doctrine to Congress December 2, 1823.

It required considerable courage for Monroe to make the pronouncement, as there was great doubt the meager resources of the United States were adequate to prevent any of the powers of Europe from swallowing up the new nations in the Americas. But none of the governments of Europe felt inclined to test Monroe's determination. Almost twenty years went by before foreign powers seriously considered annexing a part of the Americas, and by that time the military strength of the United States was a considerable deterrent.

President Monroe's foresight and courageous action probably preserved the independence of a number of the young, struggling nations in South America. Indirectly, the Monroe Doctrine also served to isolate the United States from the quarrels and alliances of Europe, so that America remained unhampered in her development.

"Liberty and union,
now and forever, one and inseparable."

(Daniel Webster, 1830)

The American Colonies all united against the British in the Revolutionary War. For a long time after the United States government was organized there was serious debate as to whether it was a government to be dominated by states' rights or a government of national union.

By 1830 the economic interests of the country made for sharp divisions between New England, the South, and the West. The South claimed that the national government was a confederacy of independent states. Some Southern leaders, led by Henry Clay, began agitation to have the South withdraw from the Union.

Admittedly a partisan New Englander, Daniel Webster usually devoted his energies to issues that favored the North. Webster was also perhaps the best known orator in the United States, at a time when public oratory was recognized as a great talent. With one of the most forceful speeches he had ever made, Webster addressed the United States Senate on January 26, 1830: "Liberty and Union, now and forever, one and inseparable!" His impassioned plea had a great influence in playing down Southerners' efforts toward withdrawing from the Union.

"I'll call her 'Old Glory,' boys, 'Old Glory'!"

(William Driver, 1831)

There are differing accounts of the origin of the term "Old Glory" as a designation of the United States flag. The version usually believed authentic concerns the sailor, William Driver, who later became a sea captain. As Driver embarked for a voyage around the world in 1831, a group of his friends at Salem, Massachusetts, presented him with an American flag.

In his enthusiasm for the gift, Driver hoisted and unfurled the flag, shouting, "I'll call her 'Old Glory,' boys, 'Old Glory!"

American ■ 25

The original flag, to which Driver gave this designation, remained with his descendants until 1922. In that year the flag was placed on display at the Smithsonian Institution in Washington, D.C.

"To the victor belongs the spoils."

(William Learned Marcy, 1831)

United States government employees had no civil service standing when the government was first organized. State employees likewise had no protection, and could be replaced whenever a new candidate was elected to office.

Commenting on this situation in a Senate speech in 1831, Senator Marcy of New York pointed out that: "Some politicians ... claim, as a matter of right, the advantages of success. They see nothing wrong in the rule that to the victor belongs the spoils...."

Modern civil service laws did not got into effect until long after Marcy's speech (until 1883 in fact). But Marcy had brought the problem to the attention of the public and to the agenda of all political parties.

"Our Union, it must be preserved!"

(President Andrew Jackson, 1832)

In 1828 the United States Congress passed a tariff that required the payment of stiff duties on textiles, glass, earthenware and paper brought into the United States.

The Southern states seethed with resentment at this law, as they had few factories and needed imports. Under the leadership of Vice President John C. Calhoun, the state of South Carolina called a legislative convention that declared the Federal tax law null and void. It was declared unenforceable in South Carolina.

Shortly after this time Andrew Jackson was elected to a second term as President of the United States. Many expected that Jackson would compromise in some way with the Vice President and with the determined stand of the Southern states that had helped to elect him.

There was no compromise, however on such a serious issue with Jackson. He realized that individual states could not be allowed to tell the national government what to do in any situation. In a post election banquet Jackson raised his glass in a toast; he uttered six brief words: "Our Union, it must be preserved." (He is sometimes quoted as saying, "Our Federal Union, it must be preserved!")

Later Jackson told Secretary of State Edward Livingston, "The Union must be preserved, without blood if this be possible, but it must be preserved at all hazards and at any price." By this determined stand, many observers thought Jackson had averted a Civil War.

"Marshall has made his decision, now let him enforce it."

(President Andrew Jackson, 1832)

The government of the United States was set up on the idea that the three branches of government would serve as checks and balances on each other. Never an admirer of the United States Supreme Court, President Andrew Jackson was usually a strong advocate of states' rights.

In 1831 a crisis arose between the Supreme Court and the State of Georgia. In 1832 the court, led by Chief Justice John Marshall, struck down some provisions of Georgia laws aimed at restricting the rights of Cherokee Indians living in that area. These rights had been guaranteed previously by a treaty with the Federal government.

After the Supreme Court declared part of the Georgia law to be unconstitutional, the state of Georgia went right ahead in enforcing the invalid law. Newspaper sources quoted President Jackson as saying, "Marshall has made his decision, now let him enforce it."

Shortly after this time, the legislature of South Carolina passed a series of laws that stated in effect that South Carolina could flout any ruling of the United States Supreme Court and could ignore any Federal law. This was too much for Jackson. He became enraged. He introduced a bill into Congress that would have allowed the President to take over the state government of South Carolina. The bill never came to a vote. South Carolina and Georgia quickly backed off from any opposition to Federal courts or laws, and the matter died.

"Tippecanoe and Tyler too."

(Whig political slogan, 1840)

In the national presidential election of 1840, Martin Van Buren was the Democratic candidate. Realizing that they might have a better chance of winning with a popular military figure, the opposing Whigs decided on William Henry Harrison (1773-1841).

The Whigs pictured Van Buren as a dandy and an aristocrat who wore silk stockings. Harrison was pictured to the voters as a rough frontiersman who was accustomed to overcoming hardships. He was also described as a military hero who lived in a log cabin like many of the voters. Actually, Harrison had led United States troops against an Indian chief called "The Prophet," who had been incited by the British to attack United States settlers on the frontier.

The presidential campaign was something of a circus, with free cider, popular bands, and torchlight parades. Little was said about the qualifications of the candidates. The Whigs wanted to run John Tyler as Vice President. They also made much of the defeat of "The Prophet" by Harrison at the battle of Tippecanoe. Actually, the battle of Tippecanoe was little more than a skirmish. The Whigs nevertheless used it in their slogan, "Tippecanoe and Tyler too."

"Fifty-Four Forty or Fight!"

(William Allen, 1844)

By 1840 both England and the United States wanted undisputed ownership of the Oregon Territory. Both nations had good claims, by exploration, by settlement, and by treaties, but hundreds of American settlers began to settle in the Williamette River valley, just to the south of the Columbia River.

An almost constant stream of settlers from the Eastern states began to look for free land in the West. In a Senate speech in 1844, Senator William Allen of Ohio coined the slogan "Fifty-Four Forty or Fight!" He meant the U.S. should agree with England to divide the Pacific Northwest along the line of 54° 40' north latitude—the present southern tip of the Alaska Panhandle. Although the United States and England eventually compromised at the 49th parallel, the popularity of the slogan probably gave United States diplomats impetus to obtain a large amount of land in the final settlement.

"What hath God wrought?"

(Samuel F.B. Morse, 1844)

After seeking money for a telegraph line for about ten years, Samuel F.B. Morse was finally given $30,000 for construction of a line from Washington, D.C., to Baltimore in a Congressional appropriation. The experimental line was built between the U.S. Supreme Court room at the Capitol and a small parkway in Baltimore. On May 24, 1844 Morse stood among a crowd of curious onlookers and tapped out his message: "What hath God wrought?"

"This is the place."

(Brigham Young, 1847)

Members of the newly organized Church of Jesus Christ of Latter Day Saints, commonly called "Mormons," lived around Kirtland, Ohio. In 1831, a considerable number of this group moved to Jackson County, Missouri. There, persecution by their neighbors, and the murder of Joseph and Hyrum Smith, forced them to flee.

Traveling westward on the instruction of their leaders, the Mormons joined in the stream of people seeking new homes in unsettled areas. Thousands assembled on the west bank of the Mississippi, near present-day Omaha, Nebraska, and in April, 1847, began a trek across the Great Plains, arriving near present-day Salt Lake City, Utah, in July. Some pulled handcarts through the entire journey. When on July 24, 1847, following his scout's reports, the Mormon leader, Brigham Young, looked down into the Great Salt Lake valley, he reportedly said, "This is the place; drive on."

"A woman's place in society marks the level of civilization."

(Elizabeth Cady Stanton, 1848)

Born in 1815, Elizabeth Cady (1815-1902) received an education usually available only to gifted young men from wealthy families. Thereafter, she studied law under her father, Judge Daniel Cady, but was refused membership in the bar and the right to practice law on account of her sex. In 1840 Elizabeth Cady married Henry Stanton, who shared with her an interest in the antislavery movement. That summer they went to London where a world antislavery convention was to be held. There, Elizabeth Cady Stanton met Lucretia Mott and other women delegates from America, but all women were refused admittance to the convention hall.

On returning to the United States Elizabeth Cady Stanton made a home for her husband while he studied law. Subsequently, they moved to Seneca Falls, New York, where Henry Stanton practiced law, and where on July 19, 1848, with Lucretia Mott, Susan B. Anthony, and a handful of other women, Elizabeth Cady Stanton launched the modern women's rights movement. Her keynote address summarized specific sexual inequalities. "A woman's place in society marks the level of civilization," she declared. From 1869 to 1890, she served as the first president of the National Woman Suffrage Association.

"I would rather be right than President!"

(Henry Clay, 1850)

Henry Clay of Kentucky was one of the leading American statesmen for forty years, first as a Congressman and later, Senator. The opinions of Clay, Daniel Webster, and John C. Calhoun largely controlled Congress in the second quarter of the 1800's.

Clay was nominated for the presidency of the United States on three occasions, in 1824, in 1832, and again in 1848, and perhaps no man ever aspired to election more eagerly than he. Always, Clay seemed to work untiringly to achieve harmony and preserve union between the states, so that he became known as "The Great Compromiser." But he was not always seeking the easy way out. In 1850 Clay delivered a speech in which he declared himself against slavery. Friends warned that this speech would forever ruin his chances of becoming President, but he delivered it, anyway, including his famous statement, above.

In the last years of Clay's life, it appeared that tensions over slavery would result in a breakup of the United States, but Clay's leadership helped work out a compromise that lasted over 10 years. As he fought to preserve the Union, Clay told Congress, "I know no North — no South — no East — no West!"

"Go West, young man, and grow up with the country."

(Horace Greeley, 1851)

John Babson Soule, writing in the Terre Haute, Indiana, *Express* in 1851 used the phrase, "Go west, young man." Many young men from the eastern and midwestern parts of the country had already taken these words to heart in the decade that had gone before. Many of these were young, single men who streamed westward to prospect, trade furs, file homestead claims, or simply explore.

Horace Greeley, one of the most influential newspaper editors of that time, added to Soule's words by writing, in the *New York Tribune,* "Go west, young man, and grow up with the country."

Founder and owner of the *Tribune,* Greeley wrote: "In God's good time this is to be a land of real freedom, where equal laws shall banish rebellion, treason, and riot.... I hardly hope to live to see that day."

"Blood is thicker than water!"

(Josiah Tatnall, 1859)

In June, 1859, vessels of the British and French were attacked by Chinese along the River Peiho, in violation of agreements to permit peaceful trade with the Europeans. Although the United States was technically neutral in the matter, Captain Josiah Tatnall (1795-1871) of the United States Navy quickly brought his vessel to the assistance of the European ships, allowing the British and French to escape destruction.

It was a time when there seemed to be no central authority in China, with the whole mainland under the control of marauding bands of brigands.

When asked by American authorities to explain how he got involved in aiding his European "brothers," Tatnall pointed out that the Chinese had no responsible government, had violated their agreement, and that in addition, "Blood is thicker than water!"

"From log cabin to White House."

(traditional)

To some observers, one of the striking differences between the Old World of Europe and the New of America was the contrast between social stratification in each location. By custom in Europe it was almost impossible to rise above the social class of one's birth.

This stratification by social classes was often ignored in the New World. In America, a man of humble birth could rise to the level of his ability and accomplishments. Time after time, men born to poor, under-privileged families became leaders in business, science, or government.

Thus it was that a remarkable number of the men elected to the office of President of the United States had been born in a crude log cabin on the western frontier. News sources coined the phrase, "From log cabin to White House."

"The melting pot."

(traditional)

America was always a land that welcomed the oppressed, those persecuted because of religion, or those looking for a better opportunity in the New World. By the 1880's immigrants were coming in such numbers that America was known as "the melting pot," mixing many backgrounds into a common citizenship.

No symbol represented the hopes and yearnings of those arriving from Europe more graphically than the Statue of Liberty, designed and constructed in New York Harbor by the French sculptor Fredric Bartholdi.

In 1883 Emma Lazarus wrote a sonnet entitled "The New Colossus" to commemorate the dedication of a monument to Bartholdi; it included the famous words, "Give me your tired, your poor, Your huddled masses yearning to breathe free...."

"Nothing succeeds like success."

(John Collins Warren, 1846)

In October, 1846, Dr. John Collins Warren (1778-1856), a leading surgeon, performed the first operation in which an anesthetic was used. Ether was the substance used to anesthetize the patient for the removal of a tumor of the neck. Already one of the founders of the Massachusetts General Hospital as well as of the American

Medical Association (AMA), Dr. Warren was a leader in new techniques.

Understanding full well some of the perils in the use of an anesthetic, Dr. Warren remarked after the successful operation, "Nothing succeeds like success."

"There is a sucker born every minute!"

(Phineas Taylor Barnum, mid 1800's)

P.T. Barnum (1810-1891), America's most famous showman, mixed good-natured hoaxing with some of the most sensational attractions ever placed on exhibition.

Barnum was credited with saying "The American people like to be humbugged," and as a result of this quote he became known as "The Prince of Humbug." He was also called "Brazenmouth Barnum." Organizing the circus until it became known as "the greatest show on earth," Barnum was instrumental in transporting it by railroad car. Barnum also acquired an African elephant of great size, giving it the name Jumbo. After showing this animal in the United States, the word "jumbo" came into common usage.

A student of human psychology, Barnum frequently stated, "There is a sucker born every minute."

"Cotton is king!"

(James Henry Hammond, 1858)

James Henry Hammond (1807-1864), senator from South Carolina, was a rabid secessionist and a champion of the South. "Cotton is king!" proclaimed Hammond in a March 1858 impassioned speech in the Senate to explain the Southern economy. He emphasized that any attempt to curb the production of cotton would be a serious blow to the Southern farm economy.

But after the Civil War, Southerners realized the need to diversify their economy. Henry Grady, nationally prominent editor of the *Atlanta Constitution,* spoke for the new spirit of the South in a speech on December 21, 1886, saying: "The old South rested everything on slavery and agriculture, unconscious that these could neither give nor maintain healthy growth."

"The only good Indian is a dead Indian."

(Philip Henry Sheridan, 1859)

Major General Sheridan (1831-1888) was one of the three highest ranking generals in the Union forces during the Civil War. He was highly regarded as a fighting man and as a commander.

After graduation from the United States Military Academy at West Point, in 1853, Sheridan served for several years as a cavalry officer in wars against the Indians. He was still only a lieutenant when the Civil War broke out.

Because of his deadly fights with the Indians, Sheridan seemed unable to see any justice in the Indian's complaints against white settlers or the white man's government. Sheridan was quoted by the newspapers of his time as saying, "The only good Indian is a dead Indian."

"A house divided against itself cannot stand."

(Abraham Lincoln, 1858)

Abraham Lincoln made a speech to the Illinois Republican Convention in Illinois that nominated him as its candidate for president, on June 16, 1858. Some say that this speech elected him President. Lincoln said: "If we could first know where we are, and whether we are tending, we could better judge what to do and how to do it.... A house divided against itself cannot stand. I believe this government cannot endure permanently half slave and half free. I do not expect the union to be dissolved; I do not expect the house to fall; but I do expect that it will cease to be divided...."

"On to Richmond!"

(popular Union cry, 1861)

As the Civil War began in April, 1861, President Abraham Lincoln called up militia regiments from the loyal states. Rash Northern sympathizers told one another that the Confederate rebellion would be crushed in a single battle, that the country would be back to normal by harvest time.

While troops were being called up, President Lincoln could stand at the rear of the White House and see the Stars and Bars of the Confederacy flying from the heights on nearby Arlington. But most of the Northerners refused to take the problem seriously. "On to Richmond" (Capital of the Confederacy) became the popular cry.

During July, 1861, Union troops tried without success to clear the roads south of Washington of Confederate troops. Months passed before the Northern armies actually had much strength. The local press, reflecting the restiveness of a people eager for results, and convinced that the Confederacy had no real support, continued the cry, "On to Richmond!"

On July 16, General Irvin McDowell left Washington with 35,000 Union troops, intending to march deep into the Confederacy. Some Washington newspaper correspondents called McDowell's green troops "the greatest army in the world." But McDowell knew better.

On July 21, McDowell's forces attacked a smaller Confederate army under Southern General P.G.T. Beauregard at a little Virginia stream called "Bull Run." For a time it appeared that McDowell would win, but the determined Confederate volunteers under "Stonewall" Jackson held fast. Eventually, Beauregard was able to mount a counterattack. The Northern retreat became a rout. It was worsened by a traffic jam of carriages belonging to newspaper men and Northern congressmen who had come to see the fight.

Bull Run became a symbol for disastrous defeat. It emphasized the emptiness of the cry, "On to Richmond!" The people of the country had been almost totally ignorant of the demands and sacrifices that would be necessary to win a war.

"There stands Jackson, standing like a stone wall! Rally around the Virginians!"

(Barnard E. Bee, 1861)

Thomas Nathan "Stonewall" Jackson (1824-1863) has sometimes been called the best officer who served under General Robert E. Lee in the Civil War.

In the first battle of Bull Run, July 21, 1861, at a small creek near Manassas, Virginia, Jackson took the lead by standing firmly while others wavered. To encourage his own men, General Barnard E. Bee shouted, "There stands Jackson, standing like a stone wall! Rally around the Virginians!" After that time, Jackson was known as "Stonewall Jackson."

Accidentally shot while scouting at dusk, Jackson was killed in 1863.

"He will regret it but once, and that will be continuously."

(James Ewell Brown ["Jeb"] Stuart, 1861)

The call to arms beat like an alarm bell throughout both the Confederacy and the Union as young men flocked to join the colors. Civil War pitted brother against brother and friend against friend, in bitter rivalry. Many of the most distinguished officers who fought against each other had been classmates and friends at West Point.

In 1855 James Ewell Brown Stuart, known as "Jeb" Stuart (1833-1864), a young officer under the command of General Philip St. George Cooke, 2nd United States Dragoons, had married the

General's daughter, Flora Cooke. With the outbreak of war, General Cooke remained with the Union Army, even though he was a native of Virginia. But "Jeb" Stuart and General Cooke's own son joined the forces of the Confederacy. "Those mad boys. If only I had been there" was General Cooke's comment on learning his son and son-in-law had joined the Army of Virginia.

Disappointed and surprised that General Cooke had refused to come to the aid of Cooke's native Virginia, "Jeb" Stuart countered, "He will regret it but once, and that will be continuously."

As the war dragged on, "Jeb" Stuart rose through the ranks to become one of the most celebrated generals in the Confederate cause. But eventually, Stuart was mortally wounded and died a few days later, in 1864, in the arms of Flora Cooke Stuart.

As Stuart lingered, knowing death was near, he never indicated regret in serving the cause that had divided the loyalties of his family, as well as those of an entire nation.

"To git thar fustest with the mostest."

(Nathan Bedford Forrest, 1861)

Confederate cavalry general Nathan Bedford Forrest (1821-1877) was one of the most effective and daring generals in the Civil War. When the Rebel leader was asked the secret of his success, he was quoted as saying that it was "to git thar fustest with the mostest." Some said that Forrest used the frontier language with which he was most familiar. But to the newspapers he used perfectly good English.

"I can't spare this man, he fights!"

(President Abraham Lincoln, 1862)

Throughout early years of the Civil War, President Abraham Lincoln raised one general after another to command of the Union armies. In battle after battle the Northern generals had superiority in manpower, munitions, transport, and supplies, but each general consistently failed to win the victories needed to defeat the Confederacy.

Among the Union commanders was the dashing George McClellan (1826-1885). Looking every inch the soldier, McClellan was still reluctant to engage unless every conceivable advantage was on his side. It was this indecision that caused Lincoln to tell his cabinet, "I would like to borrow McClellan's army, if McClellan himself has no use for it."

McClellan was finally forced to fight by General Robert E. Lee's invasion of the North at Antietam. But he was so timid he allowed Lee to escape from a position that seemed a near-catastrophe for the South.

After McClellan, Lincoln promoted General Ambrose Burnside, who is remembered for having the most imposing set of sideburns* in the Union army. Burnside was almost as inept as McClellan. Lincoln then tried "bombastic" John Pope, "Fighting Joe" Hooker, who never quite lived up to his name, and General Meade.

Lincoln also promoted other generals, men like General H.W. Halleck, who then spent all his time at a desk, issuing false reports that criticized General U.S. Grant, who was one of his subordinates. In order to protect his own reputation with the press, Halleck incorrectly reported that serious Northern losses at the battle of Shiloh had been caused by Grant's ineptitude. Lincoln's Cabinet, swayed by popular demands, asked for the removal of Grant. But officers sent in by Lincoln to investigate indicated that Grant had actually commanded with distinction.

In April, 1862, tired of false charges and of generals who would not fight, Lincoln told his Cabinet, "I can't spare this man [Grant], he fights!"

Never was there a general who looked so unlike a dashing hero as Grant (1822-1885). But he continued to justify Lincoln's confidence, winning a major victory at Vicksburg and hammering out other triumphs.

On March 2, 1864, Lincoln had Congress designate Grant a lieutenant general, saying, "Thank God I have found a general at last!"

---

*These side whiskers were in fact named for Burnside, by switching syllables.

"Shoot, if you must, this old gray head,
but spare your country's flag!"

(attributed to Barbara Frietchie, 1863)

During 1863 an account in the *Atlantic Monthly* related this story of Barbara Frietchie (or Fritchie, as it was sometimes spelled): citizens of Frederick, Maryland, began to pull down their United States (Union) flags as Confederate troops of General Thomas J. "Stonewall" Jackson opened a drive to capture the town.

A 90-year-old resident, Barbara Frietchie, observed one of the flags being lowered as the Rebel troops came near. Grabbing the flag, even as bullets spattered nearby, Barbara Frietchie defied the Southern soldiers. The poet John Greenleaf Whittier later versified Frietchie's action as follows: "Shoot, if you must,/ this old gray head,/ But spare your country's flag, she said."

According to tradition, General Jackson came on the scene about this time, with Frietchie defying the oncoming Confederate troops. General Jackson apparently had no sympathy for any Northern sympathizers, but as he observed the old lady's spirited display, he ordered, "March on! Get back into line and march on!"

"I propose to fight it out
on this line if it takes all summer."

(Ulysses S. Grant, 1864)

In 1864, as the Civil War wound down, General Grant's Northern forces pressed steadily against the Confederates. Attempting to avoid Grant's continuing pressure, General Robert E. Lee massed his troops near Spottsylvania Court House, Virginia. Fighting raged on for six days, with each side losing more than 8,500 men. The Confederates stubbornly held. Fearing that his Union troops might not be able to hold up indefinitely, General Halleck in the War Department in Washington cabled his worry to General Grant on the scene. "I propose to fight it out on this line if it takes all summer," wired back the determined and aggressive Union general.

"Damn the torpedoes! Full steam ahead!"

(David Glasgow Farragut, 1864)

By August, 1864, the Union navy had succeeded in blockading all the ports of the Southern Confederacy except three. Of these three (Wilmington, Charleston, and Mobile) Mobile may have been the best guarded. The harbor was reached by a narrow inner passage under the powerful guns of Fort Morgan. Inside were several Confederate ships, and the whole inner channel was protected with mines (then known as torpedoes).

Admiral Farragut of the Union navy led a fleet of ships in an attack on Mobile, a tactic designed to help the land forces of General Ulysses S. Grant. One of the United States ships, the *Tecumseh,* disregarded orders and plowed across the minefield. Striking an explosive charge, the *Tecumseh* plunged heavily to the bottom, carrying her captain and most of her crew. Coming next, the *Brooklyn* led a column of wooden ships that began to hesitate and drift. For a few seconds it appeared the whole Union column would be thrown into confusion.

Without hesitation, Admiral Farragut gave the order, "Damn the torpedoes! Full steam ahead!" The Union ships quickly regained their positions and resumed the attack. A major victory for Farragut's forces followed shortly after.

"With malice toward none; with charity for all;
with firmness in the right..."

(President Abraham Lincoln, 1865)

Perhaps only a handful of men in all history have approached the writing of a speech with the ability of Abraham Lincoln. Few of the presidents who have followed Lincoln, especially those who have written speeches by committee, have compared with "Old Abe."

In his Second Inaugural Address, delivered March 4, 1865, Lincoln said: "With malice toward none; with charity for all; with firmness in the right, as God gives us to see the right, let us strive on to finish the work we are in; to bind up the nation's wounds; to care for him who shall have borne the battle, and for his widow, and his orphan—to do all that which may achieve and cherish a just and lasting peace, among ourselves, and with all nations."

With the Civil War coming to an end, Lincoln had the ability to forgive and to work for a better future.

"Now he belongs to the ages."

(Edwin M. Stanton, 1865)

"Sic semper tyrannis!"
«*Thus always to tyrants!*»

(John Wilkes Booth, 1865)

On the night of April 14, 1865, President Lincoln attended a showing of *Our American Cousin* at Ford's Theater in Washington, D.C. After the orchestra played *Hail to the Chief* and the performance began, it appeared to be just the kind of comedy the President relished.

During the second scene of the third act, the crack of a pistol was heard from the Presidential Box, as Lincoln was shot in the back of the head by an assassin.

Within a matter of seconds, a man stood on the flag-draped balustrade, brandishing a dagger. He then leaped to the stage and shouted *"Sic semper tyrannis!"* (a Latin phrase meaning "thus always to tyrants"). The wild-eyed assassin, Shakespearean actor John Wilkes Booth (1838-1865), broke his leg in jumping to the stage, but made his escape through a back door, mounted a waiting horse, and fled to Virginia. Overtaken by Federal troops while hiding in a barn near Bowling Green, Booth was shot when he refused to surrender.

On the morning of the following day, Lincoln died. In his lifetime, Lincoln had recognized ability in men, appointing Edwin M. Stanton (1814-1869) his Secretary of War, although he disliked Stanton personally. Always outspoken, several years earlier Stanton had "declined to associate with such a damned, gawkey, long-armed ape" as Lincoln. But when Lincoln died on April 15, Stanton's voice choked with emotion. "Now he belongs to the ages," Stanton said.

"Bury contention with the war."

(Robert E. Lee, 1865)

The most able generals are not always those who win — even in defeat there are some marked with the stamp of greatness.

Until Ulysses S. Grant came to command of the Army of the Potomac, late in the Civil War, no Northern general had ever enjoyed any real success against Robert E. Lee (1807-1870), a former superintendent of the United States Military Academy at West Point.

Almost all of the Northern leaders had marked superiority in men, rations, ammunition, and all the material advantages needed to win battles. But time after time, Lee and his Confederate troops had outmaneuvered and outfought the Union soldiers. After Grant was made Commander-in-Chief of the Northern armies, the weight of numbers and supplies began to tell, and Grant's relentless persistence spelled out the end of the Confederacy.

Feeling that further fighting was pointless, Lee surrendered at Appomattox Court House on April 9, 1865. Returning to the life of a private citizen for the first time in forty years, Lee became president of Washington College (now Washington and Lee) at Lexington, Virginia, to "educate Southern Youth into a spirit of loyalty to the new conditions."

In a letter to a Southern partisan, written April 15, 1865, Lee asserted: "Bury contention with the war." In other correspondence he said, "Madam, do not bring up your sons to detest the United States government. Recollect that we form but one country now. Abandon all these local animosities and make your sons Americans."

*"God reigns and the government
at Washington still lives."*

(James A. Garfield, 1865)

On the day that Lincoln died, a whole nation went into mourning. Some even feared that the government would collapse in chaos. A young Ohio Representative to Congress immediately made a speech, while away in New York City. "God reigns and the government at Washington still lives," Garfield said.

The assassination of a President, especially one of the stature of Lincoln, was a great tragedy. Garfield (1831-1881) wanted to emphasize that the government of the United States was not dependent on any one man, even Abraham Lincoln. Garfield was not in agreement with Lincoln on many aspects of reconstruction, but he said, "They slew the noblest and gentlest heart that ever put down a rebellion upon this earth."

Elected to the presidency himself in 1880, Garfield was also cut down by an assassin after four months in office. As President, Garfield had not had time to accomplish a great deal, but he had distinguished himself in the Congress prior to election.

As he lay dying, Garfield asked a friend whether he would be remembered in history. "Very definitely," was the answer that came back, "but the government will be able to carry on."

Garfield himself had expressed the basic truth in that earlier speech in New York, at the time of Lincoln's death: "One falls, and another falls.... Death does its work, obliterates a hundred, a thousand—private, captain, general, President—but the nation is immortal!"

"The last rail is laid, the last spike driven."

**(presidents of the Union Pacific and Central Pacific
railroads, 1869)**

Material progress of a people can often be measured by the development of their transportation facilities. By the time of the Civil

War there were many miles of railroad in the eastern United States. But there was still no railroad to the Pacific coast.

In July, 1865 the Union Pacific began building westward from Omaha, Nebraska, following the north bank of the Platte River. About the same time the Central Pacific began laying track eastward over the Sierras.

Eventually, on May 10, 1869, the two lines came together at Promontory, Utah, 1186 miles west of the Mississippi and 638 miles east of the up-river port of Sacramento. Leland Stanford, president of the Central Pacific and later the founder of a great university, drove the last spike. To add spectacle to the historic occasion, Stanford hammered a spike of gold (alloy) into a laurelwood railroad tie, using a hammer with a silver head.

"The last rail is laid, the last spike is driven," read the telegram signed by the presidents of the two railroads to United States President U.S. Grant, announcing the beginning of transcontinental service.

"Dr. Livingstone, I presume?"

(Henry M. Stanley, 1871)

The Welsh waif called John Rowlands spent his early years in a workhouse orphan's school at Mold, Flintshire, England, and at 17 set off as cabin boy on a vessel bound for New Orleans.

Arriving in Louisiana, he was befriended by a kindly merchant named Henry M. Stanley, who provided a home, his name, and some education. The adoptive father died without a will in 1861 when the youth was 20, once again leaving the boy to fend for himself.

Joining the Confederate army at the outbreak of the Civil War, young Henry M. Stanley (1841-1904) was soon taken prisoner. Still seeking adventure, Stanley volunteered for service in the Union Navy and was an ensign on the ironclad *Ticonderoga*.

At the close of the war, Stanley went to Turkey, Asia Minor, and Abbysinia, winning a reputation as an outstanding journalist for the *New York Herald*.

It was at this time that the Scottish medical missionary, David Livingstone (1813-1873), was active in exploring the wild continent known to the outside world as "darkest Africa." Livingstone had caught the imagination of the entire English-speaking world, and was a symbol of the fight to stop the slave trade. But he had not been heard from for more than two years. Yet, because of Livingstone's thirty years' work among the tribes, any mail addressed to him anywhere in Africa would eventually reach the doctor.

In 1869 Stanley accepted a commission from the *Herald* to establish contact with Livingstone, then obsessively seeking the source of the Congo River, in the interior of the African continent, and Stanley set out with an elaborately outfitted expedition of 192 men. Dispatches from Stanley were followed with great interest by the whole world, and Stanley himself contributed greatly to the exploration of that area.

Eventually, Stanley made contact with Livingstone at Ujiji, on Lake Tanganyika (in modern Tanzania) on November 10, 1871, giving him the famous wry greeting in so unlikely a circumstance.

"Mr. Watson, come here, I want you."

(Alexander Graham Bell, 1876)

Working as a speech teacher and therapist, Scottish-born Alexander Graham Bell (1847-1922) worked out the principle on which the telephone was based before he was 27 years old.

A confirmed inventor, Bell, by then a professor at Boston University, spent all his spare time and money working on a "harmonic telegraph" (one that would carry all the varied frequencies of the human voice) with another inventor, Thomas A. Watson. On March 10, 1876, after a couple of years of success, the two were together making numerous adjustments to their coiled springs, tuning forks, and equipment. Bell was not expecting anything out of the ordinary. But suddenly, in response to a sound from his assistant in another room, Bell said, "Mr. Watson, come here, I want you," and Watson heard him on their instrument. There were the first recognizable workds spoken via "telephone."

"War is hell!"

(William T. Sherman, 1879)

One of the more successful Northern generals during the American Civil War, William Tecumseh Sherman is even yet remembered with hatred by Southern sympathizers for his destructive march from Atlanta to the sea.

Sometimes called "the first modern general," Sherman (1820-1891) made his famous march on the premise that war can be ended sooner by destroying an enemy's ability to wage war than by killing soldiers. Following this principle, Sherman laid waste the Confederacy's heartland, burning crops and buildings, sabotaging rail lines, and taking or killing livestock. The mayor of Atlanta appealed to Sherman, but the General answered: "War is cruelty, but you cannot refine it!"

Much as Sherman's methods were condemned, they may well have ended the war with a reduced loss of lives. Perhaps the General deserved better in the minds of the Southern people. Shortly after the war had come to an end, Sherman wrote to President Grant: "I do think some political power might be given to the young men who served in the Rebel army, for they are a bettter class than the adventurers who have gone South purely for office."

Sherman, himself, never claimed any personal satisfaction from his march through Georgia. Speaking of war, he said in a national address: "Its glory is all moonshine. It is only those who have neither fired a shot nor heard the shrieks and groans of the wounded who cry aloud for blood, more vengeance, more desolation. War is hell!"

"Our Constitution is color-blind,
and neither knows nor tolerates classes among citizens."

(U.S. Supreme Court Justice John Marshall Harlan, 1896)

The institution of slavery permitted mistreatment, dehumanization, and imprisonment of blacks. Slavery officially ended with the

Civil War, but consequences resulting from racial deprivation have persisted ever since. The granting of freedom was a necessary step, but the black race was still without those educational tools and facilities needed to bridge the gap in educational and economic differences.

One of the landmark decisions handed down by the courts in this civil rights struggle was that of Plessy v. Ferguson (163 U.S. 537), decided in 1896. In that case the United States Supreme Court held that states could compel racial segregation in the use of public facilities, provided equal facilities were available to all races. In a sharply worded dissenting opinion, Justice John Marshall Harlan condemned the majority decision in the Plessy case. "Our Constitution is color-blind, and neither knows nor tolerates classes among citizens," Harlan declared. But in spite of Harlan's impassioned plea, the "separate but equal" concept continued to be the law until 1954.

In the famous case of Brown v. Board of Education of Topeka (347 U.S. 483), the United States Supreme Court in 1954 reversed the Plessy decision. In the Brown case the court said that "separate but equal" was a contradiction, and that segregation in itself was discrimination.

In the years since the Brown decision, Federal courts all across the United States have struck down schemes designed to get around desegregation. Equality may not yet be an absolute reality, but it has been brought to the attention of the American consciousness.

"You shall not crucify mankind
upon a cross of gold."

(William Jennings Bryan, 1896)

With the discovery of silver in the Western states, the Democratic party wanted the government to permit the free coinage of silver at a fixed rate with gold. This was because most of the Western states were Democratic at that time and the usage of silver would help the West's economy. The Republicans, however stood for a continuance of the gold standard.

48 □ Famous Phrases

A delegate to the Democratic National Convention in 1896, Bryan (1860-1925) wrote the "free-silver" plank of the platform and made a speech to the convention. He said: "Having behind us the producing masses of this nation ... and the toilers everywhere, we will answer their demands for a gold standard by saying to them: You shall not press down upon the brow of labor this crown of thorns, you shall not crucify mankind upon a cross of gold."

As a result of his stirring oratory, Bryan won the Democratic nomination, but he lost the election to William McKinley. Bryan ran unsuccessfully for president three more times.

"Remember the Maine! To hell with Spain!"

(catch phrase, Spanish-American War, 1898)

On January 25, 1898, the battleship *U.S.S. Maine* was ordered into the harbor of Havana, Cuba, to protect Americans living in the area. It was a time when sentiment was building in all of Spain's New World colonies to declare their independence.

On February 15, the *Maine* was blown up while lying at anchor in the harbor, killing 260 American officers and crewmen. One of the world's most powerful ships, it was completely destroyed. No proof was ever discovered of who blew up the ship, though there were strong indications that Spain was responsible.

As relations with Spain worsened, the United States declared war. "Remember the Maine! To hell with Spain!" became the chant. United States naval forces and ground soldiers quickly won decisive victories that caused Spain to sue for peace.

"You may fire when ready, Gridley."

(George Dewey, 1898)

Commodore George Dewey (1837-1917) was known in America as "the hero of Manila." Dewey was in command of the

United States Pacific fleet when war broke out with Spain in 1898. He received orders to proceed to Manila in the Philippine Islands and seek to destroy the Spanish fleet stationed there.

With the *Olympia* in the lead, on April 30, 1898, Dewey's six ships engaged the Spanish fleet of ten cruisers and gunboats. To get at the Spanish, however, Dewey had to slip into the harbor at Manila under cover of the dark. This was because the entrance to the bay was controlled by shore batteries that had a far greater range than the largest guns on Dewey's ships.

Although the Spanish had ten ships to Dewey's six, the American ships were more modern and had bigger guns. Dewey went about the engagement quite methodically. One of the most frequently quoted phrases of the war was Dewey's famous order, "You may fire when ready, Gridley."

"I'm from Missouri."

(Willard Duncan Vandiver, 1899)

Missouri is frequently known as the "show me" state. It is not unusual to express any kind of disbelief by simply stating: "I'm from Missouri." The idea for this statement came from a speech by Missouri Congressman Willard Duncan Vandiver (1854-1932), who told of the native skepticism of his constituents in a naval banquent speech at Philadelphia in 1899, as follows: "I come from a state that raises corn and cotton and cockleburs and Democrats, and frothy eloquence neither convinces nor satisfies me. I'm from Missouri. You have got to show me."

"Be easy with him, boys!"

(President William McKinley, 1901)

Nothing has disturbed the American people more than the senseless assassinations of her presidents. William McKinley, 25th President, was the third to fall in this manner.

On September 6, 1901, McKinley held a public reception at the Pan-American Exposition in Buffalo, New York. Standing in line to shake hands with hundreds of people, McKinley was approached by an anarchist, Leon Czolgosz, who concealed a revolver in a bandage that seemed to cover an injured right hand. As the President drew near, Czolgosz shot McKinley without warning, a bullet penetrating the abdomen.

A number of soldiers were nearby, and soldiers and spectators immediately seized Czolgosz, who was in danger of being lynched on the spot.

"Be easy with him, boys!" the mortally wounded McKinley cried out, deploring additional violence and appealing to the right of every man, regardless of his crime, to have his day in court.

The President lingered for a week, then died. Czolgosz was tried, convicted and executed in the same year.

"Speak softly, and carry a big stick."

(President Theodore Roosevelt, 1901)

Theodore Roosevelt (1901-1909), 26th President of the United States, was something of a physical weakling as a young boy. Eventually, however, he molded himself into a very rugged physical specimen. In a letter he once said, "I am as strong as a bull moose, and you can use me to the limit." Continuing this aggressive posture, Roosevelt became famous as a leader of the "Roughriders" in the Spanish-American war. As a result he was one of the heroes of the famed "charge up San Juan Hill" that helped contribute to a quick end to this war.

Before he became President, Roosevelt had a slogan that he used in New York state politics; historians however cite a speech at the Minnesota State Fair, October 2, 1901, as the origin of "Speak softly, and carry a big stick." A firm believer in the Monroe doctrine to keep European nations from gaining colonies in the New World, Roosevelt used this tactic, for example, in keeping England and Germany from invading Venezuela to collect large debts owed by that country.

Whether Roosevelt would have actually gone to war to protect this hemisphere is not known, but in any event Roosevelt's known attitude persuaded the English and Germans to submit the debt collection to arbitration.

"Genius is 2% inspiration and 98% perspiration."

(Thomas Edison, 1930)

As an inventive genius, Thomas Alva Edison (1847-1931) seemed to be in a class by himself. A predecessor of our modern technical age, Edison laid the groundwork for many new devices and perfected the use of electricity for lighting.

"Edison's brain had the highest cash value in history," one reporter commented. A very modest man who worked almost incessantly to perfect his inventions, Edison himself often remarked the great difference between creativity and hard work.

"The world must be made safe for democracy."

(President Woodrow Wilson, 1917)

In August, 1914, the world was shocked by the news that Germany had invaded France. American sentiment was almost uniformly to avoid involvement in any manner, and on August 4, 1914, President Woodrow Wilson (1856-1924) issued the first of a series of Proclamations of Neutrality.

On May 7, 1915, a German submarine sank the British passenger liner *Lusitania,* and 138 American lives were lost as the ship went down. Freedom of the seas became a burning issue, and Wilson was besieged by pacifists gathering on the White House lawn to sing "I Didn't Raise My Boy to Be a Soldier," as well as by those who cried for a declaration of war to protect American shipping. For a considerable time Wilson managed to steer a course of "peace with honor."

In February, 1917, Germany resumed a policy of unrestricted submarine warfare, after a temporary cessation of this brutal activity. Within the next month a German plot to involve Mexico in a war with the United States was uncovered, and in March German U-boats sank five unarmed American ships. The patience of the country was at an end.

On April 2, 1917, Wilson asked Congress for a declaration of war. He outlined the idealistic aims of the United States:

"The world must be made safe for democracy ... its peace must be planted upon the tested foundations of political liberty.... We seek no indemnities for ourselves ... the day has come when America is privileged to spend her blood and her might for the principles that gave her birth and happiness and the peace which she has treasured. God helping her, she can do no other."

In the end, the United States joined the Allies to win the war, but Wilson believed that he had lost the peace. It was his fondest dream to see the United States as a leader in the League of Nations, an organization set up for the peaceful government of the entire world.

But congressional leaders in his own country would not subscribe to the surrender of American rights that many believed membership in the League entailed. And in his blunt, sometimes undiplomatic way, Wilson had alienated a large segment of the Congress. By some he was regarded as a dreamer, and it was not until the time of the United Nations after World War II that the United States was willing to join such an international body.

While Wilson died with his dream of unity unfulfilled, from April 2, 1917, until November 11, 1918, he swayed the whole world as few other statesmen have ever swayed it. Ever the idealist, he never doubted — "Ideas live; men die," he said.

"Lafayette, we are here."

(Charles E. Stanton, 1917)

In 1777 eleven men left France for the American colonies in a ship they had equipped themselves. These young idealists were under the leadership of the Marquis de Lafayette (1757-1834), who had left a life of riches and ease at the French court to aid the struggling American revolution. A graduate of the French Military Academy at Versailles, Lafayette gained a staff position with General George Washington. Serving without pay, and sustaining wounds, the young Frenchman became a fast friend of the American commander. Eventually, Lafayette's fighting reputation became so well known to British troops that they nicknamed him "The Boy."

When France also went to war against England, Lafayette returned to Europe in 1779, but came back to the New World the next year, as France sent a fleet and troops to cooperate with American forces. Lafayette was in charge of the Continental troops at Yorktown that helped bottle up the British commander, General William Cornwallis, in the surrender that terminated the American Revolution.

Returning to France, Lafayette was active in the French Revolution, and was Parisian commander of the National Guard after the fall of the Bastille. For nearly two years he was one of the most powerful men in France, credited with doing much to stop the excesses of the French mobs.

When United States troops arrived in July 1917 to aid the French during World War I, almost 140 years after the American Revolution, United States officials acknowledged America's debt to the French hero who lies buried in Paris under dirt from Bunker Hill. "Lafayette, we are here," said Charles E. Stanton on July 4, 1917, speaking for John J. Pershing, the American commander-in-chief, at Lafayette's grave.

Hell, heaven, or Hoboken by Christmas!"

(John J. Pershing, 1918)

General John J. "Blackjack" Pershing (1860-1948) was the leader of the American Expeditionary Forces sent to France in World War I. Intent on getting the war over with as soon as possible, Pershing was quoted by the newspapers in 1918 as issuing this optimistic and aggressive prediction (which proved correct).

"The only thing we have to fear
is fear itself."

(President Franklin D. Roosevelt, 1933)

When Franklin D. Roosevelt (1882-1945) took office in 1933, the United States was mired in the most severe economic depression that had ever gripped a nation of free enterprise. Some were standing in soup lines or walking the streets for any kind of job. Others had experienced business failures, while many had lost the savings of a lifetime through bank foreclosure. People were experiencing real want, and the moral fibre of a whole nation had sagged.

Roosevelt was elected on the promise that he would bring the country a "New Deal." He immediately proposed a series of untried economic measures to relieve the paralysis. Some of these new ideas were probably unsound, and some were unconstitutional, as the Supreme Court informed the President. But still other legislation under Roosevelt's programs seemed to put the country on the road to economic recovery.

Whether one disagreed with Roosevelt's unorthodox methods, there were few who doubted that he brought hope to a nation thirsting for encouragement, as he declared in his first inaugural address, March 4, 1933, "The only thing we have to fear is fear itself."

"This generation of Americans
has a rendezvous with destiny."

(President Franklin D. Roosevelt, 1936)

As a leader, Franklin D. Roosevelt pointed out that America had only to believe in her own greatness. In accepting the Democratic party's nomination for a second term as President, Roosevelt told the country:

"There is a mysterious cycle in human events. To some generations much is given. Of other generations much is expected. This generation of Americans has a rendezvous with destiny...."

"One World"

(Wendell L. Willkie, 1940)

The story of Wendell Willkie (1892-1944) was the simple, "Horatio Alger like" story of an Indiana farm boy who climbed to financial success and great popularity.

Willkie was Republican party candidate for President of the United States in 1940. This was at a time when the United States, under President Franklin D. Roosevelt, was on the brink of World War II. Willkie did not agree with a great deal of Roosevelt's political philosophy. There was also opposition to the election of any man (Roosevelt) to the presidency for a third term. Based on his ability and popularity, and on the third-term issue, Willkie did better than most people expected, but still lost heavily.

Both before and during World War II, Willkie realized the importance of keeping the United States united, in facing world problems and in military affairs. Consequently, Willkie's oft-repeated slogan, "One World," contribute considerably to the strength of America.

"The arsenal of democracy"

"The 'Four Freedoms'"

(President Franklin D. Roosevelt, 1941)

By January, 1941 the fires of conflict burned all over Europe, and the black clouds of war loomed large in America. President Roosevelt was convinced that if the "island fortress" of Britain fell to the armies of Nazi Germany, that Hitler would never be satisfied until he achieved mastery of the Western world.

Short of an actual declaration of war, Roosevelt believed the United States should give all possible aid to England, describing his country as an "arsenal of democracy." He therefore persuaded Congress to pass a bill authorizing the leasing or lending of war materiel to countries fighting the Axis powers. Fifty overage destroyers were given to England almost as soon as the bill was passed.

In his January 6, 1941, message to Congress asking for passage of the Lend-Lease measure, Roosevelt outlined the idealistic aims of the United States to help create a better world by enumerating "Four Freedoms" that should serve as goals for all countries. Later, speakers in many nations referred to Roosevelt's four freedoms as the ideals for which the United Nations were fighting. Roosevelt listed these freedoms as follows:

"(1) The first is freedom of speech and expression — everywhere in the world.

(2) The second is freedom of every person to worship God in his own way — everywhere in the world.

(3) The third is freedom from want — everywhere in the world.

(4) The fourth is freedom from fear — everywhere in the world."

"Remember Pearl Harbor!"

(traditional, 1941)

About 7:45 a.m., Sunday, December 7, 1941, Japanese planes without warning struck the American fleet lying at anchor at Pearl Harbor, Hawaii. Many of the United States warships did not have steam up, and almost all were easy targets in the clear morning light. The flagship *Arizona* was badly damaged, and many others were completely lost or crippled for months. Much of what had been a proud, effective fleet was sunk or reduced to a mass of blackened, smoking metal.

The people of the United States reacted to the attack with a wave of fury and outrage. The Japanese treachery had occurred even while diplomatic officials of the highest rank were arriving in Washington for the stated purpose of beginning peace talks. The next day President Franklin D. Roosevelt told the Congress: "No matter how long it takes to overcome this premeditated invasion, the American people, in their righteous might, will win through to absolute victory!" The cry, "Remember Pearl Harbor!" was taken up by the whole nation, as a reminder of the event that had precipitated war.

"a date that will live in infamy!"

(President Franklin D. Roosevelt, 1941)

The American people were not prepared for war, either in their own minds or with their weapons, at the time of the Japanese attack at Pearl Harbor that began American involvement in World War II. But once the people were aroused, they fought magnificently. On December 8, 1941, the day after Pearl Harbor, President Franklin D. Roosevelt spoke for a united, angry people when he asked Congress to declare war: "Yesterday, December 7, 1941—a date that will live in infamy—the United States of America was attacked by naval and air forces of the Empire of Japan...." Instead of serving as "the arsenal of democracy," the United States was plunged into active participation to preserve the democratic way of life.

"Sighted sub—sank same."

(Donald Francis Mason, 1942)

In the early months of World War II there was little news that cheered the American people. Japanese land and naval forces were sweeping across almost all of the Pacific. Nazi submarines appeared to sink American ships almost at will. Looking for signs of hope until America's industrial might could be brought to bear in the war effort, the home front was greatly heartened by a simple, laconic communication from the armed forces. "Sighted sub—sank same" was the radio message from United States Navy pilot Donald Francis Mason to his base on the Atlantic coast, January 8, 1942.

"I shall return."

(Douglas MacArthur, 1942)

In the opinion of some, General Douglas MacArthur (1880-1964) was the greatest military man of his time. Others regarded him as a pompous, conceited, egotistical officer who would brook no orders from anyone. But he never ran from a fight.

Overwhelming numbers of Japanese soldiers landed in the Philippines almost as soon as World War II began. The invaders steadily pushed the Americans and their Philippine allies down the Bataan Peninsula. United States supplies were very short, and soon troops were near starvation. Rations were cut in half, and were halved again, and still the Japanese pressed on. The American troops, many of them National Guardsmen from New Mexico, continued to fight with great bravery. But eventually they were starved into surrender at Corregidor.

Before the surrender came, MacArthur had received orders to leave for Australia, to assume command of the Pacific Southwest Sector. But he refused to leave his sick and starving troops, who were still resisting. On March 10, 1942, MacArthur received an order from President Roosevelt he could no longer refuse.

On the night that he left the Philippines for Australia, MacArthur told the world: "I came through, and I shall return." He went to Australia by PT boat and by Flying Fortress from the coast of Mindanao. His phrase, "I shall return," became a favorite war slogan. On October 20, 1944, MacArthur's forces invaded the Philippines, the General wading ashore with his troops, fulfilling his promise.

"Scratch one flattop!"

(R.E. Dixon, 1942)

The pure air, bright sunlight, and transparent water of the Coral Sea in the Pacific, May, 1942, made it a beautiful site for the first naval battle in history in which no ship on either side sighted the other.

The Japanese navy, with uninterrupted victories from the time of Pearl Harbor, pressed on across the Pacific under Vice Admiral Takagi, toward the intended occupation of Australia. The Japanese force included the fast aircraft carriers *Shokaku* and *Zuikaku,* along with other powerful ships. American units under Admiral Fletcher included the aircraft carriers *Lexington* and *Yorktown.* A United

States scout plane reported two Japanese carriers and four heavy cruisers about 175 miles northwest of the American force. Fletcher, quite naturally assuming this to be Takagi's strike force, ordered the launching of full deckloads of planes. Actually, the message from the observation plane had been either sent or decoded incorrectly, since it should have read "two heavy cruisers and two destroyers." This meant, of course, that a great part of Fletcher's strength had been sent toward the wrong target.

But by good luck, some of the American planes chanced upon the Japanese light carrier *Shoho,* which was sunk after only ten minutes of furious attack. "Scratch one flattop!" radioed Lt. Commander R.E. Dixon of the *Lexington*'s dive bomber command. A short time later the *Lexington* was engaged and sunk by Japanese planes. But in the end the battle was a standoff. At that juncture the increase in American planes and ships began to tell, and the war in the Pacific took a turn for America and her allies.

"Sighted aircraft carrier. Am trailing same. Please notify next of kin."

(P.B.Y. pilot, Midway, 1942)

The Japanese naval and land forces dominated the war in the Pacific until the battle of Midway in June, 1942. In this momentous air and naval struggle, the Japanese power was turned back for the first time.

The last message radioed by one slow P.B.Y. plane was sent by the American pilot: "Sighted aircraft carrier. Am trailing same. Please notify next of kin." The pilot knew that he had little chance against an aircraft carrier, but he had no choice.

"The hopes and prayers of liberty-loving people everywhere march with you!"

(Dwight D. Eisenhower, "D-Day" 1944)

In World War II the Allied nations agreed that resources and manpower were not sufficient to fight an all-out war in Europe and the Pacific at the same time. While progress was made in the Pacific, most of the United States effort was funnelled toward Europe. The Nazis were driven out of North Africa as Allied air and ground strength built up, and England stood firm under load after load of German bombs. Russia, meantime, beaten almost to her knees, managed to absorb much of Hitler's furious assault with the help of great courage and vast quantities of American supplies, guns, and equipment.

Then, in steadily increasing numbers, the big American and British bombers dropped "block busters" on Hitler's factories. Gradually, the tide turned, but Hitler continued to hold hostage many of the democratic peoples of Europe. When the Allies had at last husbanded sufficient strength to assault Hitler's so-called "impregnable European fortress," D-Day began, June 6, 1944.

The remaining strength of Hitler's armies were still a formidable obstacle. But General Dwight D. Eisenhower, the supreme commander, knew that help would come from all the people of occupied Europe, and, as he said in an address to Allied troops that morning, that "the hopes and prayers of liberty-loving people everywhere" marched with them.

"Go forward, always forward!"

(George S. Patton, Jr., 1944)

General George S. Patton, Jr. (1885-1945), was a colorful and daring master of United States tank warfare in World War II. The General was continually under criticism back in the states and in Europe because of his off-the-battlefield statements and actions. But there was no one who fought with more brilliance.

Himself completely unpredictable, Patton outguessed the German generals whenever they met, pressing across France. A few days before Christmas, 1944, General Gerd von Rundstedt began the last Nazi offensive. With the allies lacking air support because of bad weather, the Germans quickly trapped 10,000 United States troops near Bastogne, Belgium.

Urging his tanks and armored units to "Go forward, always forward," Patton led the columns of his Third Army as they wheeled north from the Saar. Smashing von Rundstedt's southern flank with amazing rapidity, Patton's troops liberated their trapped comrades. The tide at Bastogne was quickly turned, and the end of Hitler's Third Reich was near.

"Nuts!"

(Anthony C. "Tony" McAuliffe, 1944)

In December, 1944, the decline of Hitler's Third Reich seemed close at hand, but his armies could still deal out terrible punishment. General Gerd von Rundstedt scraped together 24 German divisions, including 10 Panzers, and the American First Army had spread itself too thinly in pursuing the Germans along the Ardennes front in France and Belgium.

Sudden snow storms cancelled out American supremacy in air support, and suddenly the powerful Nazi Panzer divisions punched two deep holes, splitting the American front into three parts. To add to the confusion, German commandos, dressed as Americans and driving captured tanks, slipped among the United States troops, surprising and killing as they went.

At the little town of Bastogne, American airborne troops under the command of General Anthony McAuliffe were cut off and surrounded by the surging Panzer army. With his soldiers dying and suffering, but hanging on desperately, McAuliffe realized Nazi power would be seriously damaged if he could hold the position until American armor and airpower turned the tide.

In answer to a German demand for surrender, McAuliffe cabled the simple word "Nuts!"; his troops held on with little to sustain them but grim determination. Eventually, the tide turned when Patton's army arrived to reinforce the troops.

"The only limit to the realization of tomorrow will be our doubts of today. "

(President Franklin D. Roosevelt, 1945)

As World War II drew to a close, the health of President Franklin D. Roosevelt gradually worsened, but his boundless optimism never failed. On the day before his death, on April 12, 1945, Roosevelt wrote another of his speeches reaffirming his confidence in America:

"...the only limit to the realization of tomorrow will be our doubts of today. Let us move forward with strong and active faith."

"My God, what have we done?"

(Robert Lewis, 1945)

Captain Robert Lewis, copilot of the American B-29 bomber, the *Enola Gay,* placed a one-line entry in his log as the first atomic bomb fell on the city of Hiroshima, Japan, August 6, 1945.

Lewis reported later that it seemed the entire area had disappeared. "My God, what have we done?" was Lewis' awe-stricken notation after the bomb had fallen. The atomic age had begun, and the impact would reverberate far beyond Hiroshima, and for a long time to come.

"Praise the Lord and pass the ammunition."

"There are no atheists in fox holes."

(traditional, World War II)

During World War II American clergymen made a heroic effort to give spiritual comfort to soldiers of all religious faiths. Living under all kinds of battlefield conditions, the chaplains and other clergy were often in as much danger as anyone else. According to tradition, one clergyman was in the midst of a battle where soldiers were struggling fiercely to keep ammunition supplied to the guns. Seeing the need for help, the clergyman entered into the act. "Praise the Lord and pass the ammunition," was his reported admonition to the troops.

Another phrase that was heard in World War II was the saying of the foot soldiers who were forced to take cover in whatever fox holes they could dig: "There are no atheists in fox holes."

"Kilroy was here."

(traditional, World War II)

The American infantryman in World War II sometimes left his mark on the war-torn buildings and walls of the European battlefield. "Kilroy was here," he wrote, scratched or painted.

Nobody really knows whether there actually was a Kilroy at the start of these inscriptions. But countless soldiers knew that they were wrapped up in the anonymity and enormity of war, and all wanted to leave their mark. Collectively, this became their way.

"The buck stops here."

"The decision was mine alone."

(President Harry S Truman, 1945)

In the summer of 1945 the country was still locked in a bitter struggle with the Japanese. As President, Truman was given the option of using the newly devised atomic bomb. According to his account, "I asked the Chiefs of Staff for their judgment and estimate of ... how many lives — American and Japanese — it would cost to invade the main island of Japan. ...I then made my final decision. The decision was mine alone."

Apparently the President did not decide to use the bomb without considerable thought. As Truman put it, "Any weapon that kills — large or small — is evil when in the hands of a killer."

On August 6, 1945, the bomb was dropped on Hiroshima. The "age of the bomb" had arrived for the entire world. No one could seriously contend that Truman had used the power capriciously or without due regard to the capabilities of the bomb. In all likelihood the total number killed in World War II had been greatly reduced. Truman was condemned by some, but thanked by a great many.

On his desk during part of his administration, Truman had a small sign that said "The buck stops here." He made it clear that all matters needing decision which had been passed along, or "bucked" by his subordinates, would be firmly decided by him. One of the most difficult decisions ever facing a President of the United States was whether to unleash the devastating power of the atomic bomb. Truman faced the question with forthrightness and courage.

"I cannot believe that God plays dice with the cosmos."

(Albert Einstein, 1950)

In 1915 Albert Einstein (1879-1955) propounded the theory of relativity, which was one of the greatest scientific achievements in history. This discovery laid the basis for the practical application of atomic energy. A reporter with a hazy idea that Einstein's theories meant there was no real order in scientific laws or in the universe itself questioned the great scientist. Everything he had propounded only reinforces the idea of order in the universal scheme, explained Einstein: "I cannot believe that God plays dice with the cosmos."

"Old soldiers never die..."

(Douglas MacArthur, 1951)

General Douglas MacArthur was one of the most able leaders of United States forces in World War II, and in the occupation and reorganization of Japan following this war. MacArthur's gallantry, fighting skill, and ability to command made him a great hero of the American people.

Over the years, however, MacArthur began to make statements that were not in conformity with foreign and military policy set by the President and by officials of the United States Department of Defense. Eventually, in April, 1951, President Truman had little choice but to relieve MacArthur of his command. Returning home for the first time in 14 years, MacArthur was acclaimed as a great hero. All the honors accorded to him were richly deserved. But when he could not accept orders from his commander in chief, he had outlived his usefulness. Invited to address a Joint Session of Congress, MacArthur recounted some of his experiences and philosophies. "Old soldiers never die, they just fade away," he said as he stepped into retirement.

"They did not know when to quit."

(President Harry S Truman, 1953)

Thirty-third President of the United States, Harry S Truman served from 1945 to 1953. Asked if he intended to run for a third term like his predecessor Franklin D. Roosevelt, Truman replied: "The trouble with too many men in public office is that they did not know when to quit."

"A people that values its privileges above its principles soon loses both."

(President Dwight D. Eisenhower, 1953)

On January 20, 1953, Dwight D. Eisenhower was inaugurated as President of the United States. In his inaugural address he pointed out that a free nation must be willing to pay for that status, adding the warning above.

"Tomorrow is now."

(Eleanor Roosevelt, 1960)

Anna Eleanor Hall Roosevelt, a world figure in her own right, was the wife of the 31st President of the United States, Franklin D. Roosevelt. With her husband restricted by infantile paralysis, she became the most active First Lady in United States history.

Though for a time, most of Eleanor Roosevelt's concerns were with family matters, they grew to embrace politics and the concerns of government. Feeling that the needs for leadership were so great that even a powerful president could not meet them all, Mrs. Roosevelt plunged herself into national issues, war problems, and the founding of the United Nations.

Never one to hold back, and believing in results, Eleanor Roosevelt said in 1960 that her motto was "Tomorrow is now."

She also commented that "You gain strength, courage, and confidence by every experience in which you really stop to look fear in the face...." She also pointed out that "Life was meant to be lived, and curiosity must be kept alive. One must never, for whatever reason, turn one's back on life."

"Ask not what your country can do for you;
ask what you can do for your country."

(President John F. Kennedy, 1961)

In his inaugural address in January, 1961, incoming President Kennedy (1917-1963) pointed out the need for unselfish devotion to one's country, and gave a newly hopeful nation an attractive and quotable slogan.

"I have a dream."

(Martin Luther King, Jr., 1963)

Martin Luther King, Jr. (1929-1968) made his famous "I have a dream" speech while standing on the steps of the Lincoln Memorial in Washington, D.C., August 28, 1963.

There had been strong civil rights leaders before King's rise to prominence—men and women like Sojourner Truth, Booker T. Washington and George Washington Carver. But a great part of society had simply not been ready to acknowledge the dignity and basic worth of the black race prior to the 1950's and 1960's.

By the force of his personality and the eloquence of his words, Martin Luther King, Jr., the winner of a Nobel peace prize, became the best-known spokesman for the expanding civil rights cause. King emphatically pointed out that "Injustice anywhere is a threat to justice everywhere."

Organizing and rallying increased support behind his cause, King told the great crowd at the Lincoln Memorial:

"I have a dream that one day on the red hills of Georgia, the sons of former slaves and the sons of former slave-owners will be able to sit together at the table of brotherhood ... that my four little children will one day live in a nation where they will not be judged by the color of their skin but by the content of their character."

King's dream has, of course, continued to expand. But King himself was the victim of a senseless murder, before his 40th birthday.

Phrases from British, French, and World History

"To go to Canossa."

(traditional, A.D. 1076)

In 1076, Henry IV (1050-1106), the so-called Holy Roman Emperor in the land that is largely modern-day Germany, was engaged in a power struggle with Roman Catholic Pope Gregory VII (ca. 1020's-1085). As a civil ruler, Henry had taken on himself the authority of appointing Church officials, a practice the Pope had specifically prohibited, and Gregory had responded by excommunicating Henry.

Soon deserted by his friends, Henry was obliged to do public penance and to pay homage to the Pope in order to retain his throne. For three days Henry stood bare-footed in the snow in the courtyard at the Pope's castle at Canossa, in northern Italy.

Finally restored to grace, Henry returned to Germany, where his princes were in revolt. Eventually, he regained political and military support of the German people, and marched on Rome. Henry then deposed Gregory as Pope and installed his own candidate, Clement III.

"To go to Canossa" has come to mean to humiliate oneself before a higher authority.

In 1872, when relations between the German government and the Vatican were strained, German Chancellor Bismarck told the Reichstag (legislative assembly), "We are not going to Canossa," as he refused to alter his position.

"I have loved justice and hated iniquity, therefore I die in exile."

(Pope Gregory VII, 1085)

Seeking revenge on a Pope who had humiliated him a decade earlier [see previous entry], Emperor Henry IV of Germany entered Rome in 1084 and installed an antipope by force. Gregory VII fled to a nearby castle and summoned Norman troops to rescue him.

These troops came, drove out Henry, and pillaged the city, then retired to the South of Italy, forcing the Pope to accompany him. At Salerno, on May 25, 1085, he died; these were his last words.

Saint Gregory was canonized in 1584; his feast day is May 25.

"Today I will kindle a fire that will illuminate the whole world."

(John Huss, 1415)

John Huss (1369?-1415) was a philosopher, priest, and teacher. Although a priest, he spoke out openly against policies and practices of the Catholic Church that he considered wrong. After a time the Pope placed a prohibition against Huss' right to speak out. Huss, however, continued to speak out because of the Pope's attempt to remove some officials of the Bohemian government and because of the worldliness of high church officials.

In 1414 Huss was ordered to appear before a council of church leaders at Constance on a charge of heresy. The Emperor gave a pledge guaranteeing Huss safety. But the Pope pressured the Emperor to ignore the pledge, and Huss was immediately thrown in jail.

Huss was placed on trial by church authorities and was not allowed to present any matters in his own defense. After a short trial he was found guilty of heresy and condemned to be burned at the stake.

Witnesses at the July 6, 1415, execution of Huss recorded his last words as he was tied to the stake: "Today I will kindle a fire that will illuminate the whole world." The Protestant church movement began almost directly as a result of the martyrdom of Huss, the movement of John Wycliffe, and the actions of Martin Luther.

"Daughter of God, you must leave your village and make your way into France"

(voice repeated by Joan of Arc, 1429)

In 1429 the hated English and their Burgundian allies occupied much of France, exploiting and plundering the countryside. Profoundly moved by the plight of her native country, the illiterate, deeply religious shepherd girl, Joan of Domrémy (1412-1431), said that she heard a voice commanding her to her king in unoccupied France.

"Daughter of God, you must leave your village and make your way into France," Joan reported the instructions. In response to this call, the unworldly, 17-year old shepherd girl (in French: Jeanne d'Arc) appeared before the uncrowned king, Charles VII. With an incredibly weak-willed king, and the French generals unable to act, Joan convinced the court that she had a divine commission to drive out the invaders. For a moment it seemed a speck of dust had caught the sun.

Bolstering the confidence of the king, Joan instilled some spirit in battle-weary troops. French soldiers under Joan's leadership raised the siege of Orleans, driving back the foreigners in battle after battle. The "Maid of Orleans," as Joan was then called, was with Charles when he was crowned king at Reims Cathedral in July, 1429.

By this time Joan believed that her mission was finished, and she asked to return to her native village. But Charles refused to let her leave with the magic she seemed to possess. About this time Charles quit sending her troops. She then fell into the hands of her enemies. Through the connivance of the English, Joan was burned at the stake as a heretic, May 30, 1431.

The spirit of liberty that Joan had kindled in her lifetime continued to burn. Other French leaders then came forward. By 1453 only the port of Calais was still in English hands.

"Along this track of pathless ocean it is my intention to steer."

"Their murmurs were in vain, as his absolute determination to reach India was unshakeable"

(Columbus, 1492)

In his journals, Columbus (ca. 1451-1506) made no secret of his intentions: "along this track of pathless ocean it is my intention to steer," he wrote. In the log that he maintained on board the *Santa Maria,* his flagship across the Atlantic, Columbus sometimes referred to himself in the third person, or as "The Admiral." (His name at birth in Genoa, Italy, was Cristoforo Colombo; he was known to the Spanish, whom he served, as Cristóbal Colón.)

Some said there were in reality two individuals called Columbus. One was a bold, practical captain. The other Columbus lived in a world of dream and illusion; perhaps he even had the gift of self hypnotism.

The unimaginative, superstitious sailors that served under Columbus on his voyage of discovery complained that they were being "dragged into a world that was no world." They feared there would never be a contrary wind that could be utilized for a passage home.

One of the men on the voyage of discovery, Hernando Colon, later reported that the mutinous crew conspired together to throw the Admiral into the sea some night when he might be "drunk with the stars."

There was no question that many of his associates could not understand Columbus, or the single preoccupation that appeared to drive him. There is little reason to believe he ever wavered in his search for the New World. In the ship's log Columbus wrote:

"The men complained of the length of the voyage and refused to go on.... [T]heir murmurs were in vain, as his absolute determination to reach India was unshakeable."

*"I will push on if we have to eat
the leather of the rigging."*

(Ferdinand Magellan, 1521)

The story of the iron-willed Portuguese Captain (with Spanish ships and crew) who first discovered a route around the world is one of the most daring chapters in the history of exploration.

With little food and water left in his tiny ships, Captain Ferdinand Magellan (ca. 1480-1521; name in Portuguese: Fernão de Magalhães) explored the southern coast of South America, looking for an opening into the Pacific. Dissatisfied with the many hardships, bad weather, and poor rations, the sailors began a mutiny. The revolt was quickly put down with the help of loyal officers and crewmen, but this incident added to the Captain's problems. But Magellan was not easily discouraged, either by opposition or by nature. In an entry in the log of his flagship, the *Trinidad,* while near the present Strait of Magellan, he wrote, "I will push on if we have to eat the leather of the rigging."

Hardships continued to mount as the explorers made their way through the rocky, dangerous straits that led into the Pacific. Three of Magellan's five ships reached the western end of the straits on March 6, 1521. But they were unable to find any fresh food until they reached the island of Guam, 99 days later. In the meanwhile a number of the crewmen had died of thirst and scurvy when supplies of water and rat-fouled biscuits ran out.

Magellan himself was killed, along with some of his crewmen, by unfriendly natives in the Philippines. The badly depleted expedition was eventually led back to Spain by Sebastian del Cano, one of Magellan's lieutenants.

The world had been circumnavigated, but at a terrible price. Of the 265 men from nine European countries who had set out on September 20, 1519, only del Cano and 17 other Europeans returned in 1522, along with a few adventurers from the Pacific islands.

"Here I stand, I can do no other."

(Martin Luther, 1521)

Martin Luther (1483-1546), friar of the German order of Eremites, changed the course of religious history.

In Luther's day it was common for a priest to post a notice on the church door of his willingness to debate a timely religious issue. On October 31, 1517, Luther nailed 95 of these arguments (theses) to the door of the little German church at Wittenberg Castle. In tacking these theses to the door, Luther's hammer split the Christian church. He had no intent to harm the established church in any way—he merely wanted to reform an evil that had become commonplace.

Luther's principal protest was against the Pope's fund raising campaign to complete St. Peter's Basilica. In exchange for a payment of money, the Pope's representatives granted an "indulgence" that excused sin automatically and freed the purchaser's soul from purgatory.

Unused to ever having his actions questioned, the Pope was incensed. He ordered Luther to recant or to be excommunicated. Given such a choice, the iron in Luther turned to steel. He answered by burning the Pope's message. "My conscience is captive to the word of God," said Luther. "I will not recant anything, for to go against conscience is neither honest nor safe. Here I stand, I can do no other. God help me, Amen."

Luther's unyielding stand led to the beginning of Protestantism. It also worked a self evaluation that took place in the parent church.

"Choose, each man,
what best becomes a brave Castillian."

(Francisco Pizarro, 1527)

Marooned on the barren dot of rock called Gallo Island, now part of Colombia, the ragged band of Spanish adventurers led by Francisco Pizarro (1475-1541) had sailed south from Panama after

76 □ Famous Phrases

hearing rumors of gold among the natives of Peru. As food ran low and storms persisted, they were soon reduced to living on crabs and shellfish.

In *The Conquest of Peru,* the celebrated American historian W.H. Prescott described the moment: "A handful of men, without food, without clothing, almost without arms, without knowledge of the land to which they were bound, without vessel to transport them, were here left on a lonely rock in the ocean with the avowed purpose of carrying on a crusade against a powerful empire, staking their lives on its success.... This was the crisis of Pizarro's fate. There are moments in the lives of men, which, as they are seized or neglected, decide their future destiny."

It was at this juncture that two vessels arrived from Panama, one carrying a letter from the Spanish governor of Panama, ordering Pizarro's expedition to return. Another letter from Almagro, one of Pizarro's supporters, urged him to remain firm in his purpose to push on to Peru. Using his sword to draw a line running east and west in the sand, Pizarro pointed to the south, "Friends and comrades, on that side are toil, hunger, nakedness, and drenching storm, desertion and death. On this side, ease and pleasure. There lies Peru and its riches; here, Panama and its poverty. Choose, each man, what best becomes a brave Castillian. For my part, I go to the south."

Pizarro and his little band pushed on, eventually accomplishing the incredible. With better weapons and hard fighting, through treachery and guile, the little band shattered the proud and intelligent Incas, reducing the native race to slavery. We have every reason to mourn now for this defeated race of Peru.

Pizarro and his Castillians did this all in the name of Christianity, but the driving force behind their action was the desire for gold and the power of conquest.

"The balance of power."

(Thomas Wolsey, early 1500's)

Thomas Wolsey (1475-1530), the English Cardinal, was one of the most influential statesmen during the reign of Henry VIII.

Wolsey considered attempts to seize territory on the continent as no longer worth the effort. Instead, he believed England should exercise "the balance of power," as he put it, rather than to seek territory for herself. According to this principle, England would throw the influence of her men and money to the weaker side, in case any nation or any ruler became too powerful.

This technique the English used for many years to counter the power of those who sought to control all of Europe.

"Do your job fearlessly."

(Sir Thomas More, 1535)

Sir Thomas More (1478-1535), hero of the modern play, *A Man for All Seasons*, was Lord Chancellor of England during the reign of Henry VIII (1491-1547). Henry is generally remembered as the ruler who divorced his Queen, Catherine of Aragon, and married five other times, as well as the king who broke relations with the Pope at Rome. While Henry played the arbitrary despot, it is doubtful whether the English people and Parliament would have followed him as they did through such momentous decisions unless the nation had firmly believed in the things Henry wanted. Beginning with the maritime power which Henry began to build up, England was on the way to her most glorious age.

Although More was Henry's principal minister, More was never in sympathy with Henry's quarrel with the Pope. A devout Catholic, More resigned in 1532 because of the divorce of Catherine.

In order to justify his actions, Henry asked many influential people throughout England to sign the Act of Supremacy, which established an independent Church of England. This More refused to do, saying his conscience would not allow approval. Henry responded by having More jailed in the Tower of London, and after 12 months More was convicted of treason.

July 7, 1535, on his way to the block, without hope for reprieve, More sensed the reluctance with which the executioner approached his task. With great dignity he told the man, "Do your job fearlessly."

"Be of good cheer, the water is coming."

(William of Orange, 1574)

In 1477 the Netherlands (Holland) won from their ruler, Mary of Burgundy (1457-1482), a document called "The Great Privilege," which granted many personal rights. Through intermarriage among the royal families of Europe, the rulership passed to Philip II (1527-1598) of Spain. A cold and unsympathetic ruler, Philip tried to take away personal rights that had been granted to the people of the Netherlands. In addition, Philip determined to force Catholicism on those who were mainly Protestant.

Spain ruled about one-eighth of the known world at the time, and had a powerful army and navy. But Philip failed to reckon with the independence and courage of the Dutch people. In 1581 most of the Dutch provinces were in open revolt against Philip. The opposition to the Spanish was led by William of Orange (known as William the Silent; 1533-1584). The war continued indecisively for approximately 80 years, with one period of truce that lasted up to 12 years.

Outnumbered and ill-equipped, the Dutch were hard pressed. Frequently unable to fight battles in the open, the Dutch stayed inside walled towns and awaited their opportunities. Valdez' Spanish troops laid siege to the important city of Leyden. The people were reduced to eating the rats in the warehouses. The mayor had sent a message to William of Orange that the food was all gone, and that the people were on the point of surrender.

Then William's troops cut the dikes that held back the sea, sending floodwaters toward Valdez' Spanish army. "Be of good cheer," was the message William sent on August 21, 1574, to Leyden by carrier pigeon, "the water is coming." In the end, the Netherlands won their independence.

"I singed the beard of the King of Spain!"

(Francis Drake, 1587)

Early in 1587 Philip II (1527-1598) of Spain began assembling warships and transports for an invasion of England. Philip detested Queen Elizabeth (1533-1603) of England. He was also tired of the raids of Queen Elizabeth's "sea dogs," who were little more than legalized pirates. Furthermore, Philip considered it his duty to force Catholicism on the English Protestants.

Realizing that an invasion was being planned, Elizabeth sent Francis Drake (1543-1596) and 30 ships to see what could be done to disrupt Philip's plans. Friendly Dutch Captains had told the English about a great concentration of Spanish shipping in the harbor at Cadiz, Spain.

With great daring, in May 1587 Drake sailed directly into Cadiz bay. Seeing what was coming, the smaller Spanish ships tried to gain the protection of the shallow part of the harbor. Philip's larger vessels braced to defend themselves. But the Spanish had clearly been taken by surprise. Many of Philip's ships did not have full crews on board, and the others were no match for Drake's men in gunnery. The element of confusion also worked to the advantage of the English. Drake's well-trained gunners played havoc, sinking some ships and setting others on fire. A few were captured and disabled or set afire.

On shore there was almost as much confusion as in the harbor. About 25 women and children were trampled to death when the gates to the fort were prematurely closed.

Remaining in the harbor, Drake continued his destruction. He sank five urcas, tub-like freighters loaded with Spanish wine, butter, dutch cheeses, and biscuits for the invading troops. By the second night the Spanish navy was able to counter-attack, sailing small fire ships toward the English fleet. Once again the sailing ability of the English came to the fore, as they successfully dodged all of the sailing torches.

When Drake had done all the damage possible, he sailed away, reporting to the Queen that he had sunk or burned 37 large ships and a number of smaller ones. In his message to Queen Elizabeth, Drake reported: "I singed the beard of the King of Spain."

After Philip had studied the matter he said, "The loss was not very great, but the daring of the attempt was very great indeed." But among Philip's ministers it was known that Drake's figures were likely correct.

But even a king's beard grows out again, and in time Philip assembled the greatest fleet ever seen, the "Invincible Spanish Armada." Drake had slowed up the Spanish, but the real fight was yet to come.

"God sent forth his breath and they are scattered."

(traditional Roman phrase, used by Queen Elizabeth, 1588)

The ancient Romans were not noted as a seafaring people. Expressing their fear of the Mediterranean, the early Romans had an old proverb: "God sent forth his breath and they [their ships] are scattered."

In 1588 Philip II of Spain (1527-1603) had assembled the most powerful fleet in history for the invasion of England. This great "Spanish Armada" consisted of 131 major warships and many smaller ones. The vessels were manned by 8,000 sailors and 19,000 marines on transports. To oppose this array, Queen Elizabeth of England (1533-1603) had a total of only 80 ships, none as large or powerful as the first line ships of the Spanish. But the English vessels were more maneuverable than Philip's warships, and some of the English mounted bigger guns.

By superior sailing and gunnery, the English sank five of Philip's larger ships at the outset, and caused two others to run aground. English fireships then caused panic among the Spanish, as vessels of the armada scattered into the North sea. A few of Philip's vessels were then picked off by the English. Most of the Spanish tried to reach home port by sailing around the British Isles. A violent storm then arose, and a number of ships were lost at sea. Other Spanish vessels ran aground on the Irish coast.

British, French, World ■ 81

All in all, the English won a resounding victory: 63 of the original great ships of the Spanish fleet were lost, while the English returned to home port with some injuries but all ships intact. A grateful Elizabeth struck a medal to commemorate the event, bearing the ancient Roman legend, "God sent forth his breath and they are scattered."

"I don't want to rule over a cemetery."

"I want every peasant to have a chicken in his pot."

(Henry IV of France, 1592)

Henry IV of France (1553-1610) was sometimes called Henry "the good" or Henry "the great." After a long struggle, he rebuilt a France that had been devastated by long wars. Much of the peasants' livestock had been driven off and killed by the warring factions.

In winning back the control of the country that he had lost, Henry laid siege to the city of Paris in 1592. The blockade around the city was not harsh, however. At times Henry allowed some foodstuffs to enter.

Asked why he did not make the blockade more effective to starve out those who still opposed him, Henry replied, "I do not want to rule over a cemetery."

When subsequently asked what aims he had for his kingdom, Henry said, "I want every peasant to have a chicken in his pot."

"Only my father could keep such a bird in a cage."

(Henry, Prince of Wales, 1603)

Sir Walter Ralegh (1552?-1618; sometimes spelling is modernized to Raleigh) has often been described as one of the most gifted and charming men England ever produced. At times a close friend of Queen Elizabeth (1533-1603), he probably fell from favor because he

82 □ Famous Phrases

had no inclination toward romance with his Queen. Nevertheless, he still enjoyed great influence.

When Elizabeth died and James I (1566-1625) became king, Ralegh was completely out of favor at court. He had been too deeply involved in court intrigue to be overlooked however, and within a short time he was thrown into the Tower of London on a charge of high treason.

Sentenced on perjured evidence of treason, Ralegh was scheduled to die. But he remained in the tower for 13 years, as James I was afraid to execute such a man on a trumped-up charge. During that 13 years, Ralegh ate well, enjoyed visits from his family, and was given a number of privileges. He passed the time by making a number of chemical experiments, by writing essays, and by completing a *History of the World*. Undoubtedly Ralegh was a man of many achievements.

In 1616, Ralegh was released to head an expedition to South America, where in defiance of King James' orders, he attacked the Spanish. On his return in 1618 he was beheaded under the suspended sentence of 1603.

The king's son, Henry, Prince of Wales (1594-1612; he never became king), had an appreciation of Ralegh's many talents. "Only my father could keep such a bird in a cage," he said shortly after Ralegh was sent to the Tower.

*"The wooden walls are
the best walls of the kingdom."*

(King Charles I of England, 1600's)

Present-day England has long relied on the Royal Navy for protection against the nation's enemies on the continent of Europe. In the present century has been added the considerable protective power of the Royal Air Force. The British Isles have remained free from foreign forces since the invasion in 1066 of William the Conqueror.

King Charles I (1600-1649) was eventually executed after he set aside Parliament and insisted on running England as he saw fit. His opposition to Parliament had finally led to civil war and to his over-throw.

Charles I, however, was one of the first English kings to see the advantages of building up the strength of the navy. He wrote: "The wooden walls are the best walls of the kingdom," referring to the wooden sides of his warships.

*"Rebellion to tyrants is obedience to God."**

(Oliver Cromwell, 1640's)

"Paint me, warts and all."

(Oliver Cromwell, 1650's)

"A larger soul has seldom dwelt in house of clay."

(Anonymous)

"A smokey soul."

(Winston Churchill)

Few of the prominent individuals in history have brought out so many conflicting judgments as Oliver Cromwell (1599-1658). Almost all of Cromwell's career consisted of his political and military opposition to King Charles I (1600-1649) of England.

In a process going back four hundred years before the beginning of Charles' reign, the English people had gained a number of personal liberties that were respected by the crown. Charles came to the throne when there was an increase in the spirit of civil liberty throughout the country, yet he attempted to do away with all liberties. In addition, control of the public purse had been given to the House of Commons, and Charles tried to do away with this right by demanding Parliament raise money for his private schemes. He then

Used as the motto on Thomas Jefferson's seal.

imposed arbitrary taxes on shipping and other private interests without asking permission of Parliament. Charles I also attempted to force his religion on the nation, and he was influenced considerably by foreign advisers.

Most of the leaders of England, other than the King, were members of the House of Commons (the lower house of Parliament). When Charles had a number of these leaders killed and when he attempted to do away with Parliament, the country rose up in arms. Oliver Cromwell was the leader of the opposition. Cromwell's statement, "Rebellion to tyrants is obedience to God," helped solidify opposition to the king.

Although he had been only a political leader up to this time, Cromwell took over the command of troops opposed to the King. Considering his lack of experience, Cromwell was a surprisingly competent military leader, especially at the battle of Marston Moor, July 2, 1644.

After his forces were routed in other battles, Charles I fled to the Isle of Wight. There, negotiations were conducted to return him to the throne, but with limitations on his power. It almost immediately became obvious, however, that Charles planned to kill his opponents after gaining power another time. As one historian said, "Charles I was probably one of the meanest and most treacherous occupants the English throne has ever known...."

The King was then taken from the Isle of Wight, convicted of treason, and executed. Cromwell apparently shared some of the responsibility for the King's execution but had not been a leader in bringing it about. Some have described Cromwell as "a villain who killed his king," or as "a dictator." Winston Churchill, who was always loyal to the monarchy, described Cromwell as "a smokey soul."

At the other extreme, he has been described as a "hero to the cause of liberty." One historian, now anonymous, said, "A larger soul has seldom dwelt in house of clay."

In his latter years a portrait painter was preparing a likeness of Cromwell, when Cromwell observed the artist touching up his work. Never one to put on airs, Cromwell ordered, "Paint me, warts and all."

Considering the nature of governments of that time, it was a terrible thing that Parliament had done in killing their King.

Undoubtedly Charles had brought many of his troubles on himself, but the English were not yet ready to do away with their monarchial form of government. The revolution had brought a more extreme conclusion than was warranted by the original quarrel. Shortly, the monarchy was restored, along with the civil rights of free Englishmen.

"The state is me!"
«L'état, c'est moi!»

(King Louis XIV of France, 1600's)

Louis XIV of France (1638-1715), known as the Sun King, reigned in pomp from age 4, in 1643, to 1715, a span of 72 years. His was the longest reign of any European monarch and came at the high point of European belief in the divine right of kings, the absolute power of a monarch.

About the time Louis' reign began Charles I was beheaded in England, and not long after came a time of major political trouble in France (the Fronde). The young King learned that authority was to be matched by power.

Cardinal Mazarin had conducted most affairs of state for the boy King but upon his death in 1661, Louis determined to bring all his ministers in subjection. He decreed that none of them could sign anything without his permission, "not even a passport."

In explanation of his state policies, Louis XIV was known to have suggested there was no state (kingdom) other than himself: "The state is me!" (or, "I am the state" as it is sometimes translated) has come to symbolize a monarch's belief in absolutism.

"If I have seen further, it is by standing on the shoulders of giants."

(Sir Isaac Newton, early 1700's)

There may be a considerable lag between the findings of a theoretical scientist and the application of those principles to the benefit of mankind. Nevertheless, scientific ideas must come before developments of a practical kind.

Toward the end of his long life, Sir Isaac Newton (1642-1727) was aware that he had contributed much to theoretical science. While not considered a vain man, Newton was practical enough to speak objectively about his achievements. Acknowledging his debt to those scientists who had gone before, Newton said: "If I have seen further, it is by standing on the shoulders of giants."

"An army, like a serpent, travels on its belly."

(Frederick the Great of Prussia, mid 1700's)

Frederick II (1712-1786), the Prussian king known as Frederick the Great, laid the foundation for the unification of modern Germany. Frederick promoted prosperity in his kingdom of Prussia by developing roads, digging canals, and by starting manufacturing. A soldier as well as an administrator, Frederick was successful in wars with the neighboring country of Austria, and added considerable territory to the Prussian state.

Recognizing the need for solving supply problems in time of war, Frederick was credited with saying that "an army, like a serpent, travels on its belly." Somewhat later, Napoleon was reported to have used a better-known version of this military truth, "An army travels on its stomach."

"After me, the deluge!"
«Après moi, le deluge!»

(King Louis XV of France, mid 1700's)

The sixty years during which Louis XV (1710-1774) ruled France marked a time of decline in national greatness. During much of this reign, Louis dispensed with his ministers, being in accord with the opinion of his predecessor and great-grandfather, Louis XIV (1638-1715), that "I am the State!" *("L'état, c'est moi!")*.

While it was a time when the French seemed to want their kings to have full authority, social conditions all over Europe were changing. Louis XV involved France in war after war, levying heavy taxes on the peasants. In addition, France lost India and Canada in these conflicts.

Of far more concern to the French peasants, however, was Louis' habit of showering huge sums of money on his mistresses, who were thought to be the real powers behind the throne. The King's complete lack of concern for the sufferings of his subjects, and his many scandals, are believed to have influenced conditions that brought about the French Revolution 15 years after his death.

But for all his faults, Louis was not out of touch with reality. He seemed aware it would only be a matter of time until a French king would be brought to task for the excesses and folly of their line. When questioned about this possibility by a member of the court, Louis is reported to have uttered the reply that made clear his callous unconcern for anything but his own pleasure: "After me, the deluge!"

"to go farther than any man had ever been before"

(Captain James Cook, 1778)

James Cook (1728-1779), the English sailor who became a British naval captain, was one of the most remarkable explorers the world has ever known. In three voyages, spanning about ten years (1768 until his death in 1779 at the hands of Hawaiian natives), Cook discovered more of the South Pacific than any other, preparing accurate maps to inform the world of his findings, and bringing back quantities of scientific data.

In explaining his motivation to the learned societies of his time, Cook stated, "I had ambition not only to go farther than any man had ever gone before, but as far as it was possible for a man to go."

"Man is born free, but everywhere he is in chains."

(Jean Jacques Rousseau, 1762)

"I do not agree with what you say, but I will defend to the death your right to say it."

(Voltaire, 1760's)

By 1750 many of the world's down-trodden peoples were looking for ways to gain personal freedoms. The French writer, Jean Jacques Rousseau (1712-1778), has been called "the conscience of this age." Napoleon said that the French Revolution would never have occurred except for the ideas presented in Rousseau's book *Social Contract,* written in 1762.

Never an active revolutionary himself, Rousseau's thoughts sometimes seemed to be clouded by the mists of insanity. Nevertheless, his writings inspired those intellectuals who were working for freedom for the French peasants.

After a time the French King placed an official ban on Rousseau's book *Social Contract.* According to one account, another famous Frenchman, Voltaire (real name François Marie Arouet) wrote to Rousseau condemning the suppression of Rousseau's writings. "I do not agree with what you say," wrote Voltaire, "but I will defend to the death your right to say it!" (Another account attributes this phrase to Voltaire, but under different circumstances.)

In his personal life, Rousseau appeared to pass from one misfortune to another. But writing about others he said, "Man is born free, but everywhere he is in chains." Rousseau did not live long enough to see his countrymen's struggles to throw off their shackles, but he was remembered by many. Influenced greatly by Rousseau's writings, the American patriot (and transplanted Englishman) Thomas Paine wrote not many years later, "Men are born and always continue free and equal in respect to their rights."

"Let them eat cake!"

(Marie Antoinette, about 1788)

At the age of fifteen Marie Antoinette (1755-1793), the beautiful daughter of Emperor Francis I of Austria and his famous wife Maria Theresa, was married to the crown prince of France. Four years later, her husband became King Louis XVI.

Accustomed to a life of gaiety and ease, Marie Antoinette had little appreciation of the problems of the French, either the city shopkeepers or the peasants in the country.

For a time Marie Antoinette had been popular with the people, but she disregarded their feelings, and was concerned only with frivolity. She also seemed determined to spend large sums extravagantly, as those at court became richer, while the far more numerous French peasants sank into deeper poverty.

The weak king, Louis XVI, and Marie Antoinette were completely out of touch with the reality of their age. According to legend, the Queen once asked one of the King's ministers why there was unrest among the people. "Because they have so little bread," was the reply.

"Then let them eat cake!" was the alleged retort of the haughty Queen.

Whether Marie Antoinette actually made the statement is not definitely known, but it was believed by the French peasants, as the spirit of the revolution swept over all France.

Eventually, the King and Marie Antoinette fled for their lives, but were captured and returned to Paris. Marie Antoinette and her husband were both brought before the revolutionary court. They were condemned and executed on the guillotine in 1793.

"Go tell your master ... that we will leave here only at the point of a bayonet!"

(Honoré Gabriel Victor Riqueti, Comte de Mirabeau, 1789)

Social and economic conditions in France during 1789 had contributed to a time of great unrest. Honoré Gabriel Riqueti, Comte de Mirabeau (Count Mirabeau; 1749-1791) was one of those elected as delegates to the French Parliament, representing the Third Estate, or common people.

Shortly after the Parliament opened its meetings, Dreux-Breze, Chamberlain of King Louis XVI, ordered the delegates to leave the assembly at Versailles and return to their homes.

Louis XVI (1754-1793), like other kings of France, had always held life and death power over his subjects. But the time had come when the common people were determined to be bullied no longer. On June 23, 1789, when the order to disband the assembly was given, Mirabeau rose instantly from his seat. Speaking at the top of his voice, Mirabeau thundered: "Go tell your master that we are here by the will of the people and that we will not budge, even at the point of a bayonet!" (another, slightly different rendering of Mirabeau's statement).

Mirabeau's determined stand caught the King's minister completely by surprise. For a time Dreuz-Breze hesitated, undecided how this opposition should be met. As the King's minister wavered, other representatives of the common people took heart. It was only a short time after great numbers of the French were involved in their struggle to demand rights for all individuals.

Mirabeau died suddenly in 1791 of natural causes, having served as President of the National Assembly.

"When you undertake to run a revolution,
the difficulty is not to make it go;
it is to hold it in check!"

(Honoré Gabriel Victor Riqueti, Comte de Mirabeau, 1791)

Whatever were the causes of the French Revolution, the original intent was apparently to win rights from the king, rather than to overthrow the monarchy and the established order. But Louis XVI (1754-1793) contributed generously to his own downfall by failing to judge the temper of the times.

For two years after the revolution began, the men who led the uprising toiled in the belief that they were working for the betterment of their fellows. They supposed that individual liberties would be set up, and that all Frenchmen would enjoy freedom of speech and religion. During this period the most influential leaders believed these ideals could be achieved by changes in the monarchial system.

But no permanent peace could be worked out between the armed crowds in the streets and the unyielding attitude of the French King. It became more and more difficult for leaders of the movement to control the mobs. As one reporter put it, "there were, as in every crowd, heroes, monsters, and idle fools."

Gradually, the leadership was taken over by the mob, with the pent up hate of some of the basest people in the country being turned on the crown and the leaders of the movement alike. "When you undertake to run a revolution, the difficulty is not to make it go; it is to hold it in check," commented Count Mirabeau (1749-1791), one of the early leaders. Before control of the government passed back into responsible hands, 20,000 Frenchmen and Frenchwomen died on the guillotine.

Mirabeau, himself, died during the period of the revolution, of natural causes. He believed until the last that he could win individual rights and still retain the monarchy. But his prophetic last words were, "I carry with me the ruin of the monarchy."

For all of his idealism, Mirabeau was a practical man at times. In describing the realities of the age he said, "Revolutions are not made with rose water."

"The greatest of all criminals
need not be judged."

(Maximilien François de Robespierre, 1793)

At the beginning of the French Revolution there was little violence directed at the monarchy. Revolutionary leaders merely hoped to obtain some rights for individuals and some economic help for the hard-pressed peasants.

Gradually the feeling against King Louis XVI (1754-1793) and his Queen, Marie Antoinette (1755-1793), hardened. Louis tried ruthlessly to stamp out the revolt. Failing to understand the mood of his people, he could see no need for any concessions to the common people. To the contrary, Louis sent appeals to the other monarchs of Europe to send their armies to kill Louis' subjects. As the people's complaints increased, tempers changed. Eventually the King and Queen were arrested and brought before the people's tribunal.

One of the Revolutionary leaders, Robespierre (1758-1794), insisted on putting the King to death immediately. "Execute him without debate, without inquiry, without defense.... The greatest of all criminals need not be judged; he is already condemned."

Robespierre's pleading for death finally had its way with the tribunal and King Louis XVI went bravely to the guillotine on January 21, 1793, undefended, unheard. The King died, not for specific acts, but for his failings toward his people.

Robespierre himself died on the guillotine on July 28, 1794, condemned by the successors of the earlier revolutionary tribunal.

"Oh Liberty, what crimes
are committed in thy name."

(Madame Jeanne Roland, 1793)

The woman known as Madame Roland (Jeanne Manon Phlipon Roland de la Platière; 1754-1793) was one of the most influential leaders of the French Revolution. She worked unceasingly to gain liberties for the common people, and her enthusiasm and ability achieved much.

A strong supporter of reasonable moderation, Madame Roland was a member of the Girondist element; her husband Jean Marie was a Girondist minister. Eventually the Girondist group was shoved aside by the irresponsible, bloodthirsty Jacobin group, as the mob turned on almost all of their decent leaders.

Anyone who opposed the Jacobins came to be regarded as an enemy of the people, almost equally as guilty as the King himself. As one who had opposed some of the extreme measures of the Jacobins,

Madame Roland was condemned and sent to the guillotine, November 8, 1793.

As she was led to the execution, she proclaimed, "Oh Liberty, what crimes are committed in thy name!" Her husband took his own life upon hearing the news.

"It is the end that crowns the achievement."

(Charlotte Corday, 1793)

When the French Revolution broke out in 1789, Jean Paul Marat (1744-1793) was a well-known French physician. A man of rabid beliefs, Marat became a violent revolutionary, urging the Parisian mob to kill anyone in France who had a position of authority. Marat's fury increased with his influence with the mob, as he systematically set out to kill anyone who opposed him in any way. He was largely responsible, with Danton and Robespierre, for overthrowing the Girondists at the National Convention, June 2, 1793.

Charlotte Corday (1768-1793) a 24-year-old noblewoman, sided with the revolution at the outset. But she was sickened by the seemingly endless number of people, many quite innocent, who were guillotined by the mob.

Believing that Marat's death would return the revolution to a moderate course, Corday determined to kill him. On July 13, 1793, Corday broke into Marat's home in Paris, stabbing him to death as he sat in his bath.

Seized and hauled before the revolutionary court, Corday was given a brief hearing. "It is the end that crowns the achievement," she explained to the unhearing mob. After little more time for explanation, Charlotte Corday became another victim for the guillotine.

"Eternal vigilance is the price of liberty."

(John Philpot Curran, 1790)

"Eternal vigilance is the price of liberty," declaimed John Philpot Curran (1750-1817), in an election campaign in Ireland in 1790.

Curran himself never achieved world-wide acclaim. But the phrase attributed to him has continually echoed down the years.

"The sun never sets on the British Empire."

(traditional)

In 1588 Elizabethan England destroyed the Spanish Armada, considered the most imposing naval fleet in the world. Philip II of Spain had constructed and assembled the fleet to punish England. For a full century before this time, Spain had been the leading sea power of the world, planting colonies in many localities in the lands discovered by Columbus.

The destruction of Philip's Armada marked a decline of power for Spain, with a corresponding rise in the naval fortunes of England. About this time English raiders began to roam the world. And by 1596 an English squadron under Lancaster was seeking out weak points in the crumbling Portuguese empire in the east. In December, 1600, Queen Elizabeth chartered the aggressive English East India Company, and in 1607 other Englishmen founded an American settlement at Jamestown, Virginia.

Spain still had strength enough to hold the colonies that were already established in the New World. The English, however, showed no timidity in contesting the claims and maritime rights of Philip's subjects. English sailors and explorers laid claim to land after land. Driving the French army out of both Canada and, in the 1800's India, and sending settlers to many of their possessions from New Zealand to Central America to Africa to Malay to Hong Kong, the British built up the most far-flung colonial empire the world has ever seen.

With colonies so widely scattered, the British boasted that "The sun never sets on the British Empire." Today, of course, the British Empire has been replaced by the British Commonwealth, a group of independent countries associated together for their mutual advantage.

But the old phrase that "the sun never sets on the British Empire" was not completely novel when it was first used. About 500 B.C. the Greek historian Herodotus reported that the Persian Emperor Xerxes boasted that the "sun never sets on my empire."

"Westminster Abbey or victory!"

(Horatio Nelson, 1797)

"Westminster Abbey [i.e., death and burial] or victory!" was the battle cry of the great British Admiral Horatio Nelson (1758-1805) at the battle of Cape St. Vincent, February 14, 1797. In that battle the British bested the combined French and Spanish fleets.

Horatio Nelson was not slated for burial in Westminster Abbey anyway. Shot in the spine by a sharpshooter at the height of the October 1805 battle of Trafalgar, Nelson was subsequently buried in St. Paul's Cathedral, London.

"I really cannot see the signal."

(Horatio Nelson, 1801)

On April 2, 1801, in the course of the long war against Napoleonic France, the British attacked the powerful Danish fleet off the coast of Copenhagen. Admiral Parker had overall command of the operation, with Vice Admiral Nelson on the *Elephant*. After a time, Parker became doubtful of the outcome and signaled Nelson by flag to retire.

A thoroughly dedicated fighter, Nelson placed his telescope to his eye, but was reluctant to break off the fight. To his aides he said,

"I have only one eye; I have a right to be blind sometimes.... I really cannot see the signal."

Using the excuse that he was unable to observe the order from Parker, Nelson turned what may have been a standoff or even a defeat into a great naval victory.

"England expects that every man will do his duty."

(Horatio Nelson, 1805)

By 1805 Napoleon was master of almost all of Europe. He had barges assembled and provisioned, ready to send his troops across the English Channel. With only a small army, the common British folk drilled on the village green with pike and pitchfork.

The only obstacle that Napoleon could see to the success of his invasion was the British navy. The French had gone to great expense to build new ships and to obtain naval aid from the Spanish. In fact, the British could send only 23 ships of the line to join battle with the 28 French and Spanish off Cape Trafalgar.

But the British had superb training and discipline, along with the leadership of a small, unimposing man named Horatio Nelson. Many of the English seamen were press-ganged jailbirds, but some of the British captains boasted that they were each worth three Frenchmen or four Spaniards.

Before the October 21, 1805, battle Nelson sent by flag a message to his captains: "England expects that every man will do his duty." On the log of *H.M.S. Prince,* one of the vessels involved, Captain Mansfield added an additional message to his crewmen: "I shall say nothing to you of courage; I trust our country never produced a coward." After an unusually bitter struggle, the English won one of the most decisive naval battles ever fought, but Lord Nelson lay dying on his flagship, a bullet through his backbone.

There was no lack of bravery or devotion on the part of the French and Spanish sailors, who also fought with great spirit and determination. Perhaps Napoleon's officers simply did not have the experience, training, or leadership of the English.

The British victory at Trafalgar cut off Napoleon from the sea, forcing him into a purely continental military strategy. It was this strategy which eventually led to his defeat on the snow-covered plains of Russia.

"The finger of God has been over me."

"The old guard dies, but never surrenders."

(Duke of Wellington, Waterloo, 1815)

"Waterloo"

(traditional)

At the battle of Waterloo, near the Belgian village of that same name, British, Belgian, Dutch, and German forces combined in a final defeat of the French armies of Napoleon. The Duke of Wellington, British commander (1769-1852), took up a strong defensive position with the Belgian and Dutch forces. The Germans, under General Von Blucher (1742-1819), were hurrying to join forces with Wellington. Napoleon believed his best chance was to attack before the Germans could arrive.

Time after time the French pressed forward in some of the bloodiest fighting that Europe had ever seen. Although the French fought bravely, the British and allied position held. When it became evident that a supreme effort would be needed, Napoleon flung his famous "Old Guard" against the English positions. Even that failed, though only after the French had exhibited great valor and had sustained heavy losses. No one doubted that Napoleon's famous old veterans had lived up to their motto: "The old guard dies, but never surrenders."

By the time night fell, both of the armies were exhausted. About this time Von Blucher's Germans arrived after a long forced march. Their additional strength quickly turned the tide, and the domination of Europe by Napoleon had ended.

Throughout almost the entire battle the Duke of Wellington had directed his troop movements from an exposed position. His aides marvelled that he never received a scratch. "The finger of God has been over me," he explained, since 63,000 men had been killed in the three square miles around the center of his position.

Before the battle, however, Wellington apparently had some doubts about the quality of the troops that had been given to him. After a brief inspection tour he reportedly told an aide: "I don't know if they frighten the enemy, but by God they frighten me."

Nowadays when one speaks of a "Waterloo," one means a final, decisive defeat.

"The Battle of Waterloo was won on the playing fields of Eaton."

(attributed to Duke of Wellington)

Many years after the battle of Waterloo, the Duke of Wellington observed the winning effort expended by the cricket teams at Eaton. He allegedly paid tribute to his British officers at the final defeat of Napoleon, thus: "The Battle of Waterloo was won on the playing fields of Eaton," by which he meant the strong British public school tradition of striving for coordination, teamwork, competitiveness and excellence in athletics had transferred to war-making.

"God is on the side of the heavy battalions."

(Marquis de Ferte Imbault)

"Fortune is on the side of the last reserves."

(Napoleon)

Practically all generals have appreciated the power of force, either in soldiers or in guns. Marquis de la Ferte Imbault (1590-1668) expressed the idea when he said, "God is on the side with the heavy battalions."

Napoleon (see following entries) meant much the same when he said that fortune favored the side who could last put reserve troops into action.

"A people who burn their houses to prevent us from sleeping in them for a night."

"I beat the Russians every time, but that doesn't get me anywhere."

"I defeated man, but nature defeated me."

"From the sublime to the ridiculous is only a step."

(Napoleon, 1812)

Ever brash and egotistical, Napoleon Bonaparte (1769-1821; in French, Napoléon, called by history Napoleon I) claimed that he had "ennobled all Frenchmen." A man with consuming ambition, historians frequently comment that he was one of those who came to power without being fit for it. Among his sayings, Napoleon remarked, "When I see an empty throne, I feel the urge to sit down on it." So long as mankind continues to bestow greater applause on her destroyers than on her benefactors, there will likely be military dictators of Napoleon's type.

Regardless of the claims of his admirers, perhaps the military ability of Napoleon was not up to his reputation. The candid severity of history cannot refuse him a high place among those who could lead an army to victory. At the same time, Napoleon completely failed to understand the strategic concept of the Russians, who scorched the earth and destroyed their supplies and dwellings as they fell back before the powerful French armies.

Penetrating far too deeply into Russia with his force of 420,000 veterans, Napoleon's troops consistently defeated the Czar's forces when they gave battle. But time after time the defenders slipped away to the east, drawing Napoleon ever deeper. Contemptuous of the Russians, "a people who burn their houses to prevent us from sleeping in them for a night," Napoleon finally added that "I beat the Russians every time, but that doesn't get me anywhere."

Then winter came, and catastrophe fell on the hungry and poorly-clad French. Over 300,000 of Napoleon's "Grand Army" became victims of exposure, disease, and starvation. Then, too, the counterattacking Russian Cossacks, dressed for the snow, continued to cut down the stragglers. Eventually, Napoleon said that "I defeated man, but nature defeated me."

In another statement, Napoleon summarized what had happened: "From the sublime to the ridiculous is only a step."

"What is history but a fable agreed upon?"

(Napoleon)

Emperor of France, Napoleon (1769-1821) is considered by most the greatest military genius of his day, and a dominating world figure. His French troops adored him, as he led them through war after war. The common people of France usually thought of him as one of the greatest men in history, since he had brought the nation to the pinnacle of glory. But to the rest of the world, Napoleon was a ruthless, bloody conqueror.

By seizing power when he did in the late 1790's Napoleon ended the confusion that followed the French revolution and he set up new legal codes that remain the basis of jurisprudence in France today. But there was little to justify the unending wars that he brought on all of Europe for twenty years.

With a cynical view of history, Napoleon is quoted as having once said, "What is history but a fable agreed upon?"

*"The moment it was certain that the lion
had been chained, sufficient words
could not be found to damn him."*

(Madame Celeste Chateaubriand, 1815)

When Napoleon was overthrown after the battle of Waterloo in 1815, the French people appeared to have no further use for their leader. Madame de Chateaubriand expressed for them the cynicism of the people when she said, "The moment it was certain that the lion had been chained, sufficient words could not be found to damn him...."

The French had been all too willing to overlook Napoleon's tyrannies so long as he was leading their forces to the domination of Europe. When Napoleon finally lost, his faults came sharply into focus.

"Religion is the opiate of the people."

(Karl Marx, 1845)

When the Russian Revolution took place and the Bolsheviks came into power in 1917, the hand that led the people was the hand of Lenin, but the voice that urged them on was the voice of the German exile, Karl Marx (1818-1883), dead for over 30 years.

Born the son of a Jewish lawyer in the Rhineland, the parents of Marx became Christians when Karl was six. But no religious teaching made much impression on Karl Marx, and early in life he showed a rebelliousness and belief in his own infallibility that was to make him a tremendous force, many believe for worse, in the modern world.

In 1841 Marx took his degree of doctor of philosophy at the University of Jena and returned to Bonn, where he began to embrace the antireligious attitude that is an essential part of his doctrine and that of the soviet-style communism that grew out of it.

While a political exile in Paris in 1845, Marx wrote that "Religion is the opiate of the people," in an effort to explain away the power that religion brings to the lives of men. Marx pretended to be something of a prophet himself, claiming for his teaching a universal validity that no generation has yet conceded to it, and that in all probability future generations never will.

"The workers have nothing to lose but their chains.
They have the whole world to gain.
Workers of the world unite!" (paraphrased)

(Karl Marx and Friedrich Engels, 1848)

Karl Marx (1818-1883) and Friedrich Engels (1820-1895), unwelcome in their native Germany, planned to remake the world according to their own ideas. Marx wrote for a time in Belgium, in France, and later in England.

In 1848 Marx and his collaborator Engels issued a "manifesto" in London on behalf of the Communist League. This was the document on which a great deal of all communist thinking has been based since that time. The manifesto stated in part: "The history of all past society is the history of the struggle between classes.... Let the governing classes tremble before the communist revolution. The proletarians [workers] have nothing to lose in it but their chains. They have the whole world to gain. Workers of the world unite!"

Undoubtedly there was validity to Marx's claim that workers had suffered injustices at the hands of European rulers. But the communists insisted on beginning anew in a completely remade world, throwing out most of the cultural values that Western society had accumulated over thousands of years.

"Theirs not to reason why, theirs but to do and die..."

(Alfred Tennyson, 1854)

Through a blunder, an English light cavalry brigade under Lord Cardigan (1797-1868) was ordered to charge a very strong

Russian emplacement in the Crimean War, October 25, 1854. A hopeless venture from the outset, only a handful of the 600 men in the brigade survived the charge into "the jaws of death."

Alfred Lord Tennyson (1809-1892) commemorated the heroic men who had no choice in his poem, "The Charge of the Light Brigade."

A French observer of this incident, General Pierre Bosquet (1810-1861), was amazed at the unflinching obedience of the cavalry brigade. "It was magnificent, but it was not war," he said.

"Questions of the day are not decided by speeches and majority votes but by blood and iron!"

(Otto von Bismarck, 1862)

Otto von Bismarck (1815-1898) was the leading figure during the mid 19th-century period of the unification of Germany from a number of independent, jealous states. On September 30, 1862, Bismarck told the Prussian parliament (diet) that only through war could unity be brought about: "The great questions of the day are not decided by speeches and majority votes but by blood and iron."

As a Prussian statesman, Bismarck achieved his goal of German unity, using the method of war that he had advocated. Bismarck then became the first Chancellor of the new nation. With the same strong will that had marked his drive for German unity, Bismarck built up the military, economic, and political strength of the German state. By the time of his retirement, Germany was a world power to be reckoned with. He became known as the "Iron Chancellor."

Some of his policies probably helped set the stage for Germany's war with France in 1870 (the Franco-Prussian War), and likely affected German attitudes toward conquest as late as the time of Hitler in World War II.

*"It seems a pity,
but I do not think I can write any more."*

(Captain Robert Falcon Scott, 1912)

In 1911 Robert Falcon Scott (1868-1912) was in a race with the Norwegian explorer Roald Amundsen (1872-1928) to be the first to reach the South Pole.

After many hardships, and the turning back of portions of his party, Scott and his English companions set up a base camp and supply stations along the route to the pole. By late December 1911, Scott and four others made the last assault, knowing Amundsen to be at least 60 miles closer. Dragging sledges over the ice, they made slow progress in unusually heavy snow storms. When finally they made it on January 17, 1912, Scott and his four men found that Amundsen had already reached the South Pole, leaving markings. They immediately set out on the return trip. Weather conditions continued to be terrible, and one by one all five died of scurvy, cold and hunger.

Scott kept a diary throughout the trip, and his diary was found along with the bodies of his companions in a tent in which they made their last camp. The last entry in Scott's diary read: "We shall stick it out to the end, but we are getting weaker, of course, and the end cannot be far. It seems a pity, but I do not think I can write any more."

"The lamps are going out all over Europe."

(Sir Edward Grey, 1914)

In August, 1914, it was apparent to many statesmen on the European scene that "the clouds of war lay dark on the horizon." Nation after nation became embroiled in secret alliances and intrigue.

"The lamps are going out all over Europe," said Sir Edward Grey (1812-1898), the British Foreign Secretary. "We may not see them lit again in our lifetime."

"They shall not pass!"

(Marshal Pétain, 1916)

During 1916 the Kaiser's German troops launched one of the most powerful offensives of World War I near the French city of Verdun. This town was a key point in the allied line protecting Paris. German experts believed the fall of Verdun would force the French to ask for peace.

Taking over the command of the French defenses, General Henri Philippe Pétain (1856-1951) held off assault after assault by the Germans from February to November. Remaining in possession of the French troops, Verdun became the symbol of the rugged, bitter fight. Pétain was credited with uttering the simple, but stirring phrase that became the allied watchword: "They shall not pass!"

In the period between World War I and World War II, Pétain was one of the most honored military figures in the world. But when World War II came he was an old man, perhaps beyond fighting. Pétain disgraced himself by urging the French to surrender and by working as a collaborationist with the Nazis, as head of the Nazi-occupied French Vichy government. At the end of the war he was brought to trial as a traitor, convicted and condemned to death but General Charles de Gaulle (1890-1970), head of the government, commuted the sentence to life imprisonment. The contempt with which postwar French patriots treated him never completely erased the memory of Pétain's heroic stand of an earlier time.

"Bread, land, and peace."

(traditional Russian phrase, 1917)

"Bread, land, and peace," was the slogan of the suffering, oppressed Russians who fought the October Revolution in 1917 in the name of democratic, lofty ideals. The struggle against Czar Nicholas II (1868-1918) stirred a feeling of compassion in the people of many countries.

The well-meaning movement, however, fell under the control of the communists. For better or worse, the Communist Party line has always been set by a few individuals. Any dissent or criticism is regarded as nothing less than treason. Leon Trotsky (1879-1940), one of the early schemers in the takeover of Russia said, "the majority is not counted up, but pressured over."

The major revolutionary leader, V.I. Lenin (1870-1924), built a practical political machine but had no method for keeping it subordinate to the good of the Russian masses. Nor is there any reason to believe that he had any concern for the feelings of the Russian people. Lenin and his followers drove many of the kulak class (Russian peasants) from their homes where they died by the thousands from starvation and cold. Their only crime was being in disagreement with revolutionary decrees.

The corruption of the revolutionary aim, the disenchantment with the idealism, is a familiar theme in many revolutionary movements throughout history. Lenin claimed that the results he would achieve justified the means he used. He said, in effect, that evil is justified in achieving desirable ends—that even tyranny in the name of the people will eventually result in freedom.

The Russians had already risked their lives in the Revolution for "bread, land, and peace," but Lenin refused to give them the freedom they had won. The Russians have not yet shaken off the Communist yoke which replaced that of the Czar.

"My left yields; my right is broken through; situation excellent; I attack!"

"The best means of defense is to attack!"

(French Marshal Ferdinand Foch, 1918)

Marshal Ferdinand Foch (1851-1929) was one of the French heroes of World War I. A daring, aggressive fighter, at the decisive battle of the Marne River in 1918, Foch said, "My left yields; my right is broken through; situation excellent; I attack." (Some accounts give a slightly different wording of this phrase.) About the same time Foch explained, "The best means of defense is to attack."

British, French, World ■ 107

"Even the walls have ears, comrade!"

(traditional Russian phrase, 1930's)

By the treaty of Brest-Litovsk, signed with Germany in March, 1918, Russian participation in World War I ceased. But bitter class war raged on in Russia for three years. Thereafter, sporadic revolts against the harsh governments of Lenin and Stalin (1879-1953) flared into the open with regularity. Secret factions sprang up in all sectors and secret informers appeared to be everywhere.

Entire classes of people that opposed the socialistic ideas of government, such as the prosperous peasants, the kulaks, were deported to forced labor camps, by the thousands, or shot down by Russian troops.

In the Communist Party, Stalin purged all opposition, with staged public trials where it suited his purpose, or secret executions of others who opposed him. Some, who were merely relatives of Stalin's political enemies, were sent to concentration camps, the "salt mines" of Siberia.

In this fearful time, the Russian people, afraid to confide in anyone, repeated a phrase to the outside world that told their plight — "Even the walls have ears, comrade!"

"Peace with honour."

"Peace in our time."

(Neville Chamberlain, 1938)

In 1938, the leader of the British government, Neville Chamberlain (1869-1940), brought the English people to the brink of annihilation. Confused by a mingling of foolish, unreal dreams, Chamberlain paid no attention to the warnings of such persons as Winston Churchill (1874-1965).

A confirmed pacifist, Chamberlain was faced with difficulties in the Mediterranean that had been created by the Spanish Civil War. Chamberlain negotiated a treaty with Fascist Italy whereby England recognized Italy's taking of Ethopia on condition that Italy withdrew troops from the Spanish conflict.

Shortly after, Chamberlain accepted an invitation to confer with Hitler at Berchtesgaden, Germany. Nattily dressed, with his ever-present rolled-up umbrella, Chamberlain left without the king's permission to leave the country, resenting also Parliament's questioning of his reasons for going. Bowing to pressure from Hitler, who threatened to start a war, on September 30, 1938, Chamberlain signed the so-called "Munich Pact." In that document he agreed not to oppose Germany if Hitler appropriated certain areas of Czechslovakia. Upon his return home, Chamberlain called this capitulation to diplomatic blackmail as having obtained "peace with honour." He also called it "peace in our time."

It appeared not to bother Chamberlain that he had bargained away parts of several countries and that he had allowed Nazi Germany to swallow up large territories, without even so much as raising his voice in protest. For his part, Hitler intensified efforts to built up his armies. "Today Europe, tomorrow the world," was the slogan of the German army.

About a year later, on September 1, 1939, when Hitler considered his armies ready, Germany invaded Poland. France and England were forced into the war to honor their defensive alliance with Poland. By this time it was obvious to even the most confirmed pacifists that "peace in our time." was a foolish dream. Those who held contempt for Chamberlain derisively referred to him as "the man with the umbrella," after his appearance during the much photographed flight to and from Germany.

"Blitzkrieg"
«Lightning war»

(traditional)

The three Punic Wars (264-261 B.C., 218-201 B.C., and 149-146 B.C.) were bitter struggles between Rome and Cathage. In the end, the city of Carthage was completely destroyed and all Carthaginian territory annexed to the Roman Republic.

During the First Punic War, which ended indecisively ("a peace that was no peace"), the young Carthaginian general Hamilcar fought brilliantly. With only moderate support from the Carthaginian government, it has been theorized that Hamilcar's forces would have administered a lasting defeat to the Romans.

Due to the suddenness with which Hamilcar attacked, a writer of that time commented that he merited his title of *Barca,* which in the language of the Carthaginians meant "lightning" (in German, "Blitz").

The title was added to Hamilcar's name, and to all succeeding generations he has been known as Hamilcar Barca, father of the even more famous general, Hannibal.

At the beginning of World War II, as the powerful armored columns of Nazi Germany drove across Europe almost unhindered, a new German term came into world consciousness: *Blitz* ("lightning") and *Kreig* ("war") combined as *Blitzkrieg.* Thus the Germans and the world described the lightning-like attack, reminiscent of the tactics of Hamilcar Barca, more than 2000 years before.

"The 'Phony War'."

(historians of World War II)

When Hitler's Panzer divisions invaded Poland without provocation in September 1939, England and France were obligated to come to the aid of their Polish ally through a treaty of mutual defense.

Months of inactivity in the west followed the outbreak of war. The Germans were intent on cleaning up opposition in Poland, and on conquering Norway and Denmark. Relatively weak in armies and supplies, the French and English worked to build up their strengths. They also waited attack behind the supposedly impregnable Maginot Line, which stretched across much of France.

In England, citizens made black out curtains for their windows, but air attacks never came.

As inactivity continued, the press and the people on the street came to speak of the military situation as the "Phony War." But the inactivity was of comparatively short duration. In May, 1940, Hitler's armored troops swept around the end of the French defensive line. France fell almost before the English could realize their peril.

"I have nothing to offer but blood, toil, tears, and sweat!"

(Winston Churchill, 1940)

In early 1940, with a long and bloody war ahead, with England standing almost completely alone against Nazi Germany, and with invasion expected on a day to day basis, Prime Minister Winston Churchill (1874-1965) rallied the English people with magnificent speeches in Parliament, like this one (House of Commons, May 13, 1940):

"I have nothing to offer but blood, toil, tears, and sweat. We have before us an ordeal of the most grievous kind. We have before us many, long months of suffering and struggle. You ask what is our policy? I will say: It is to wage war by sea, land and air, with all our might and with all the strength that God can give us; to wage war against a monstrous tyranny, never surpassed in the lamentable catalogue of human crime.

"That is our policy: You ask, what is our aim? I can answer in one word: Victory—victory at all costs, victory in spite of all terror, victory however hard and long the road may be; for without victory there is not survival!"

"This was their finest hour!"

(Winston Churchill, 1940)

On April 9, 1963, United States President John F. Kennedy conferred honorary American citizenship on a foreign statesman that Kennedy described as "half American and all English"—Sir Winston Churchill (1874-1965; his mother was American by birth). Paying well-deserved tribute to the great Allied leader from World War II, Kennedy said, "In the dark days and darker nights when England stood alone—and most men save Englishmen despaired of England's life—he mobilized the English language and sent it into battle. The incandescent quality of his words illuminated the courage of his countrymen."

Coming to office in 1940, with no time to prepare for World War II, Churchill rallied the British people with some of the most memorable prose ever uttered. On June 18, 1940, Churchill had warned Parliament that Nazi invasion appeared to be inevitable. "Let us therefore brace ourselves to our duties and so bear ourselves that, if the British Empire and its Commonwealth last for a thousand years, men will still say, 'this was their finest hour.'"

"Never in the field of human conflict was so much owed by so many to so few!"

(Winston Churchill, 1940)

After the German Panzer (tank) divisions overran France, Hitler turned his attention to the planned assault on the British Isles. Boats and barges were assembled by the Germans, numbering into the thousands. They were placed all along the Dutch, Belgian, and French coasts, ready for the invasion. The British air force, of course, bombed these assembly areas as often as possible. Yet it still appeared that the German concentrations would be overwhelming.

The British home army drilled and waited, but the Nazi invasion never came. Hitler had decided not to send the barges loaded with troops until the German Luftwaffe (air force) controlled the skies over the English channel sufficiently to beat off the British Royal navy and Royal air force. Therefore, the first phase of the invasion would be for control of the channel and the southeast coast of England.

On August 8, 1940, Hitler ordered the epic "Battle of Britain," sending hundreds of German planes into the heaviest air attack the world had yet seen.

Outnumbered greatly by the Nazis, the Royal Air Force

(R.A.F.) pilots more than made up for the difference by their courage and ability. On a single day (August 15, 1940), out of more than a thousand Luftwaffe planes, 158 were shot down by British pilots, and 17 more German planes were lost to antiaircraft fire. The R.A.F. lost only 34 planes, with 17 of their pilots parachuting to safety.

For three months Hitler's intensive attacks continued, both night and day. In the end it was the Germans that could not keep up the pace. By November 1, 1940, the Nazis abandoned daylight raids, and with this change came the abandonment of immediate plans for the invasion of England.

Seven months of intensive, terrible night bombings were still to follow. But the R.A.F. had already saved England. Winston Churchill (1874-1965) paid tribute to the men of this valiant air force when he said, "Never in the field of human conflict was so much owed by so many to so few!"

*"We shall fight on the beaches, we shall fight
on the landing grounds, we shall fight in the fields
and in the streets, we shall fight in the hills;
we shall never surrender..."*

(Winston Churchill, 1940)

On April 9, 1940, Hitler's blitzkrieg was turned against western Europe. The Netherlands, Belgium, and Luxembourg were the first victims of the campaign, which Hitler had promised the Germans would "decide the fate of the German nation for the next thousand years."

The Nazi Panzer (tank) divisions, accompanied by waves of Stuka dive bombers, quickly crushed the Low Countries. Then the Germans turned against France. Breaking through in the weakly defended Ardennes Forest, which the French had considered impassable for major troop movements, Hitler's armored divisions cut France in two. All the British troops on the continent were pinned in a pocket along the coast of France, in a trap that grew smaller by the hour.

By the "miracle" of the evacuation from the beaches of Dunkerque (or Dunkirk, as the British call it), the British Royal Navy saved all but 30,000 of the 350,000 British troops and got them back to England.

All the strength of the outnumbered Royal Air Force (R.A.F.) was concentrated in the area to give air cover against the powerful Luftwaffe (German air force). But neither navy nor air force could have ferried the troops across the English Channel without the help of hundreds of English volunteers, using almost every kind of boat to be found in England. Nearly 700 private vessels, from giant liners to unseaworthy motorboats were pressed into service. As the boats reached Dunkerque, the British troops waded out shoulder deep to board the rescue craft. All the while bitter air battles raged over head, as the makeshift armada made trip after trip.

But only the British troops could be returned. Their heavy guns, tanks, and most of their rifles had to be abandoned in France.

To outside military observers it seemed unlikely that Britain could survive very long thereafter. Winston Churchill (1874-1965) rallied the British people with yet more great speeches: "we shall defend our island; whatever the cost may be, we shall fight on the beaches, we shall fight on the landing grounds, we shall fight in the fields and in the streets, we shall fight in the hills; we shall never surrender, and even if, which I do not for a moment believe, this island or a large part of it were subjugated and starving, then our Empire beyond the seas, armed and guarded by the British fleet, would carry on the struggle."

"The children can't go without me — I can't leave the King, and of course the King won't go."

(Queen Elizabeth, 1940)

Day after day German bombers came over London in the fall of 1940, dropping a steady rain of bombs. This was the period of the blitz, as historians call it. Queen Elizabeth (1900-), consort of the reigning monarch George VI (1895-1952), was asked by her subjects why she did not find a safer place in the country. The Queen explained, "The children can't go without me—I can't leave the King, and of course the King won't go."

This was at a time when Prime Minister Winston Churchill (1874-1965) had just warned the English people that Nazi invasion was imminent. Churchill had said, "You can always take one with you," meaning an invading soldier.

King George VI said he had no intention of going to the country, as he was practicing his marksmanship and would defend the street barricades as long as he lived.

"If Hitler invaded hell, I would make at least a favorable reference to the devil...."

(Winston Churchill, 1941)

As World War II seemed nearer, the Russian government of Joseph Stalin carried on secret negotiations in turn with the British, the French, and Hitler's Germany. The Russians, then militarily extremely weak, were looking for any possible way to avoid war.

During this period the British thought they were closely allied in a defensive arrangement with the Russians against Germany. But in one of the most surprising diplomatic turnarounds in modern history, the Soviet Union signed a nonaggression treaty with Germany, August 23, 1939.

Feeling that he now had nothing to worry about from the Russians, Hitler ordered German troops to invade Poland, September 1, 1939. As part of the pact, Germany had agreed to partition Poland with the Russians. Soviet forces invaded Poland from the east on September 17, 1939. By September 28th only mopping-up operations remained from the dismemberment of Poland.

After the fall of Poland, Hitler invaded the Low Countries and France, and the French sued for peace at Compiègne, June 22, 1940.

Hitler hesitated for another year, poised to invade Britain, which proved impossible because of the unexpected power of the Royal Air Force. Instead, the Nazis turned to the east, invading Russia (despite their treaty) on June 22, 1941. At last the British had an ally.

British statesmen had good cause to be suspicious of promises that the Russians made. But Winston Churchill could see the great potential of the Russian effort. Asked if Britain could cooperate with Stalin, Churchill said, "If Hitler invaded hell, I would make at least a favorable reference to the devil."

"I have not become the King's First Minister to preside over the liquidation of the British Empire."

(Winston Churchill, 1942)

In one of his many stirring speeches, at a time early in World War II when Britain was suffering numerous defeats around the world, Winston Churchill (1874-1965) repeated his determination to win out against Nazi Germany: "I have not become the King's First Minister to preside over the liquidation of the British Empire" (to the House of Commons, November 11, 1942).

"How many divisions has the Pope?"

(Joseph Stalin, 1943)

In a series of conferences during World War II, the leaders of the Allied nations sought to coordinate their strategies for crushing the German Nazis, the Italian Fascists and the Japanese. In meetings at Teheran, Casablanca, Yalta, and Potsdam, the Allies continued their strategies and endeavored to solve the problems of the coming peace. There were great differences in outlook among the Allied leaders. Seldom was there complete agreement between Franklin Roosevelt, Winston Churchill, Joseph Stalin, or Roosevelt's successor, Harry S Truman.

When leaders from the English-speaking nations tried to convince Stalin of the Pope's worldwide influence for good, the atheist Stalin (1879-1953) scoffed. "How many divisions has the Pope?" he asked.

"Quisling"

(World War II)

Vidkun Abraham Quisling (1887-1945), a Norwegian politician and governmental official, assisted the Germans in planning the Nazi invasion of Norway in 1940. After the German landing on April 9, 1940, Quisling used his authority to hasten Norway's collapse. Thereafter, Quisling was installed as the collaborationist head of the government of occupation.

Quisling was convicted as a traitor and shot after the fall of Nazi Germany. The term *quisling* has come to be synonymous with traitor in many of the languages of the world.

"The Iron Curtain."

(Winston Churchill, 1946)

In March, 1946, Sir Winston Churchill made a speech on the campus of Westminster College at Fulton, Missouri. Perhaps the most famous phrasemaker of his age, Churchill was no longer the political leader of Britain (itself no longer an empire but part of a commonwealth). Speaking as a "citizen of the world," Churchill denounced the "iron curtain" that Russia had drawn across the Soviet Union and those other countries under Russian domination.

The curtain of secrecy and censorship set up by the Soviets was appalling to many. Churchill's descriptive slogan was widely adopted in the noncommunist world.

"We will bury you!"

(Nikita Khrushchev, 1956)

Nikita Khrushchev (1894-1971), the shrewd, vulgar but colorful, even likeable Soviet premier from peasant stock, used very emphatic words and gestures in his political speeches, never more than when blasting away at the Western world for its faults, though he coined the phrase "peaceful coexistence." His crude imagery led to some memorable lines, such as his mid-fifties warning to the West: "We will bury you." He is also famous for taking off his shoe and pounding the podium with it while addressing the United Nations in the fall of 1959.

He was turned out of office unwillingly but nonviolently in 1964 and lived in peaceful retirement until his death in 1971.

Phrases from
Ancient History

"The face that launched a thousand ships."

"Achilles' heel."

"A Trojan horse."

"Beware of Greeks bearing gifts."

We can relate only what the poets and dramatists of ancient Greece have told us to prove the actuality of the fall of the famous Greek city of Troy. The archaeologist Heinrich Schliemann (1822-1890) found ruins that fit the geographic location, and an inscription of Pharaoh Ramses III of Egypt stated that "the isles were restless" about 1196 B.C., while the ancient Roman writer Pliny spoke of a Ramses "in whose time Troy fell."

The story of this memorable city may be a skillful mixture of fact and fiction, but the traditions associated with it have become so interwoven into literary and historical lore that they have molded thinking since that time.

According to Homer and other Greek sources, Paris, son of the King of Troy, judged a beauty contest among three goddesses, Hera, Athena, and Aphrodite. Paris awarded the prize to Aphrodite, as she promised to find him the most beautiful mortal woman in the world.

Shortly thereafter, Paris fell in love with Helen, reputedly "a goddess in beauty among women," who was already the wife of Menelaus, King of the Greek city of Sparta. Paris carried Helen away to Troy by force.

The Spartans and other mainland Greeks swore vengeance against Paris and the city of Troy. The Greeks then set out for Troy in numerous small boats, and Helen became known as "the face that launched a thousand ships."

Arriving at the walls of Troy, the Greeks laid siege to the city for ten years. One of the heroes in the Greek assault was Achilles, who killed Hector, personal champion of the Trojans, and dragged Hector's body around the walls by chariot. Greek legend says Achilles' mother had dipped him into the river Styx to make him immune to wounds of battle, but the heel by which she held Achilles was not protected. Learning of this weakness, Paris killed Achilles by an arrow shot into this part of his anatomy. Thus, an "Achilles' heel" has come to mean the one small vulnerability in an otherwise invincible person.

Unable to break down the stout walls of Troy, the Greeks at last constructed a large hollow wooden horse. Leaving it outside the walls of the city, the Greeks took to their boats and sailed out of sight to await developments. The curious Trojans were suspicious of the horse, but reasoned that it was left as a tribute by a defeated besieger, and thought its large size was designed to challenge the Trojans' ability to take it within the walls of their city. This reasoning caused the Trojans to pull the horse into the city, and after nightfall Greek soldiers concealed inside it crept out and opened the city gates. By this time the Greek army had returned; they entered freely to pillage and burn the city.

Thus it is that any artiface or scheme for deception in time of war has been known as "a Trojan horse," and the phrase originated, "beware of Greeks bearing gifts" (in Vergil's *Aeneid*).

"Rome was not built in a day!"

(traditional)

The character of a people is often molded by the legends they cherish. No fanciful legend was dearer to the hearts of the ancient Italians than that of the founding of the city of Rome by Romulus and Remus, twins abandoned by their parents and raised by wolves. But there could scarcely have been any basis in fact for parts of the story.

Another saying that had its origins in the mists of Italian antiquity was: "Rome was not built in a day." From the standpoint of wealth, influence, military power, legal organization, engineering and commerce, there could be no disputing this statement.

The Romans built well, both in construction and in social institutions. Some historians have specified a certain date as the time when Rome fell to the "barbarians." Most historians will agree, however, that the strength and substance of the great city had been eroding over a long period.

Perhaps the English poet Lord Byron was thinking only in military terms when he wrote: "A thousand years scarce serve to form a state; / An hour may lay it in the dust."

"The handwriting on the wall."

"You have been weighed in the balance and found wanting."

(Daniel 5; ca. 539 B.C.)

Historical records reflect that the Jewish people were being held in captivity in Chaldean Babylonia in 539 B.C. According to the Old Testament story in Daniel 5, Belshazzar, the ruling son of the nominal king of Babylon (named Nabonidus), provided a great feast for his court that year, with great quantities of food and wine served in gold and silver plates and goblets that his father had taken from the Jewish temple in Jerusalem.

While the banquet was in progress, the fingers of a man's hand suddenly appeared and wrote a message on the wall of the banquet hall. Observing the strange hand without a visible body, Belshazzar's color changed, and he grew weak and trembled.

In great alarm, he called for astrologers, wise men, and sorcerers who might interpret the writing. None could do so. Then the Jewish leader came forward and read the message:

"God has numbered the days of your kingdom and brought it to an end; you have been weighed in the balance and found wanting; your kingdom is divided and given to the Medes and Persians."

That same night Cyrus the Great of Persia (560-529 B.C.) led an army that invaded the city and killed Belshazzar (Nabonidus escaped). The phrase "the handwriting on the wall" has come to mean a thing already determined but newly revealed.

"Come back with your shield — or on it."

(traditional Spartan phrase from about 500 B.C.)

For many years the small Greek city-state of Sparta ranked as one of the strongest military powers in the ancient world. The Spartan code taught that to die in battle was the highest honor. To survive in defeat was a disgrace which even a soldier's mother could not forgive. Historians in the other Greek city-states could not recall an instance where a Spartan had been taken captive while he could still lift his sword arm.

It was this rugged discipline that sustained the small band of Spartan defenders at the battle of Thermopylae and that kept Sparta free from outside domination. In the end, Sparta's narrow concentration on military prowess to the exclusion of learning and the arts, caused her national life to be somewhat empty.

Flight with the heavy Spartan shield was quite difficult. According to the tradition of that time, a Spartan matron sent out her son with the admonition: "Come back with your shield — or on it."

"The law of the Medes and Persians, that altereth not."

(Esther I; Daniel 6)

Surviving inscriptions of the mighty Persian emperor Darius I (ca. 560-486 B.C.) suggest that the role of lawgiver was the one he most fancied. Since not a single fragment of Darius' codes have survived, we cannot compare his abilities with those of other ancients. According to a number of classical accounts, the law of the Medes and the Persians was a byword for judicial incorruptibility. The Greek historian Herodotus tells of a Persian judge who was executed for taking a bribe.

The Medes and the Persians were the principal tribes in Darius' empire. According to ancient tribal law, whatever decree was signed both by the king and by his council of lords was law. Once signed the law could never be repealed, but remained unalterable.

Legal scholars in all ages since have wondered and questioned the rightness of a set of laws "that [could be] altereth not."

"Rejoice, we conquer!"

(Pheidippides, 490 B.C.)

In 490 B.C., Persian Emperor Darius I sent his armies to Greece, along with a powerful naval force. Greece was the only real obstacle in Darius' intent to rule the entire world (as then known by the Persians).

The military strength of the Greeks was made up of the small independent forces of Athens, Sparta, Plataea, and other cities. The combined forces of all the Greek cities were outnumbered perhaps 10 to 1 by the great Persian assembly. In addition, the Greek city governments habitually quarreled among themselves.

With Athens and most of the Greek cities protected by heavy stone walls (Sparta had no walls, relying on the strength of her soldiers), the Greek armies stayed concealed in the hills until the Persian forces separated. On the plain of Marathon, about 26 miles from Athens, the Athenians and their allies decided to do battle. There were about 20,000 select Persian troops in the contingent that faced the Greeks under the Athenian general, Miltiades (?540-?489 B.C.). The Persians relied heavily on archers, who fired a great shower of arrows. The Greeks, however, had heavy shields that turned the arrows, and the Greeks had better weapons and bodily strength for the hand-to-hand fighting that followed. The Persians suffered great losses and fled the field. Miltiades lost only 192 men, while the Greeks counted 6,400 Persian dead.

Knowing that some of the other Persian troops had gone to attack Athens before the battle of Marathon began, Miltiades realized the need to send news of the victory as quickly as possible. He feared that Athenian leaders might be persuaded to surrender when faced with great odds. Miltiades chose Pheidippides, a soldier known to be his swiftest runner, to carry the dispatch to Athens.

Reaching the city walls before the Persians, Pheidippides stumbled and gasped in exhaustion: "Rejoice, we conquer!" But

Pheidippides had put too much effort in his struggle to arrive before the Persians. He fell dead of a heart attack.

The dead at Marathon were buried in a mound which is still clearly visible on the plain. As a result of the battle of Marathon, the Greek world survived unconquered. It was the only place in the ancient world of that day where education, art, and learning were encouraged and prospered. Succeeding generations drew much from this Greek learning and culture. Perhaps all generations since that time have owed a debt to the Greeks at Marathon.

"Thou bitter water,
the king lays on thee this punishment."

(Xerxes, 483 B.C.)

Xerxes I (?-465 B.C.), Emperor of the Persians and son of Darius I, was perhaps the richest and most powerful ruler of his time. When some Greeks crossed over into Asia Minor and failed to submit to his rule, Xerxes set out to punish them. He also wanted to follow up on his father's plan to crush all the Greeks. Accordingly, Xerxes assembled the largest army ever brought together in antiquity. Many of his troops were well armed and trained. Still others from far provinces were little more than wild tribesmen armed with long stakes hardened in the fire.

To move such a great army across the open waters of the Hellespont (Dardanelles), Xerxes' engineers built a double bridge of pontoon boats, fastened together with planking and a covered roadway on top. As the bridge neared completion, an unexpected storm dashed it to pieces.

Greatly angered at this setback, Xerxes ordered his officials to lash the waters of the Hellespont. He then had the waters branded with hot irons as his officials chanted, "Thou bitter water, the king lays on thee this punishment because he was wronged without cause."

Xerxes' great army then rebuilt the bridge and used it to cross over into Europe. The Greeks were then faced with the gravest military crisis in their history.

"Go stranger, and to Sparta tell that here,
obeying her behests, we fell."

(Monument at Battle of Thermopylae)

"Good! Then we shall fight in the shade!"

(Dieneces, 480 B.C.)

In 480 B.C., Xerxes I assembled an army for the invasion of Greece that was estimated by the ancient Greek historian Herodotus to number more than a million men (but which modern historians feel was closer to 180,000).

Greece had never been a united nation, but was a collection of independent city-states, arrayed in local jealousies against one another. When the peril to the Greek cities became clear, Athens, Sparta, and some of the other leading cities agreed to unite against the invaders.

But time was of the essence, for it was necessary to levy troops, march them to assembly points, gather provisions, and repair defenses. The Spartans sent 300 troops, reinforced by 1,400 allied troops (Thespians and Thebans), to delay the Persian hordes while the Greek armies were assembled.

At Thermopylae, now a marshy plain, but in those days a narrow pass of about fifty feet between steep cliffs and the sea, the Spartans made their stand.

Most of the Spartan's Greek allies deserted when they learned the size of Xerxes' army. But Spartan law commanded her own troops to "stand fast and conquer or die."

Xerxes' spies, arriving in advance of his army, were amazed at the calm way in which the Spartans prepared themselves for almost certain death in their country's defense. Soon after, the main army of the Persians arrived at the pass, and Xerxes told his commander to bring any surviving Greeks to his tent that night.

But the Spartans quickly drove back the vanguard of the Persians, inflicting terrific losses. Then Xerxes sent the cream of his army, a band of 10,000 personal troops known as "The Immortals," to storm the pass. These elite troops likewise had no success against the Spartans.

Victory was finally gained by the Persians only after a traitor from one of the other Greek cities showed the invaders a route over the mountains to the Spartans' rear. Into the third day the fighting continued, before the small band under the Spartan king Leonidas was overwhelmed.

Perhaps men never fought more effectively in the defense of their homeland. A few of the Theban allies surrendered, but the Spartans died to the last man. They delayed the Persian invasion long enough, and within the next year the Greeks at Plataea won a resounding victory that saved the classical Greek world from annihilation.

According to the Theban survivors, the arrows shot at the Greek soldiers at Thermopylae were so numerous they literally darkened the sky. To this situation a Spartan warrior named Dieneces was reported to have commented, "Good! Then we shall fight in the shade!"

"Fishes live in the sea, as men do on the land; and the great ones eat up the smaller ones."

(Pericles, 436 B.C.)

Pericles (ca. 490-429 B.C.) was the leader of the government during the greatest period of Athenian history. "The age of Pericles" came to represent all that was highest in art, science, and government in that time.

Pericles hoped to make Athens a democracy, but he also wanted to make it the most powerful city-state in Greece. He worked to accomplish his objectives by peaceful means insofar as possible, but at times he went to war with other Greek cities.

Pericles was an idealist, but he was also practical. In one of his speeches he expressed the realism of his time: "Fishes live in the sea, as men do on the land; and the great ones eat up the smaller ones."

"We throw open our city to the world..."

(Pericles, ca. 432 B.C.)

As a statesman, Pericles always tried to run an open, above-board government. This was in furtherance of his idea of making Athens a democracy in fact as well as in theory. When questioned about the possibility that his "open society" could be taken advantage of by foreign spies, Pericles responded in a famous speech:

"We throw open our city to the world, and never by alien acts exclude foreigners from any opportunity of learning or observing, although the eyes of an enemy may occasionally profit by our liberality."

"It was as if the spring had been taken from the year."

(Pericles, 431 B.C.)

In the great Peloponnesian War (431-404 B.C.), the powerful Greek city-states of Athens and Sparta engaged in a bitter, destructive war. Losses by both sides were terrible. At a ceremony for the young men who had fallen during 431 B.C., Pericles spoke one of the most poignant funeral orations ever recorded in antiquity. "It was as if the spring had been taken from the year," he said.

"These are the walls of Lacedaemon [Sparta]."

(Agesilaus II, 398 B.C.)

During the fourth century B.C., practically every city of any importance in the civilized world had massive stone walls. Perhaps the only exception was the Greek city of Sparta (also called Lacedaemon).

Agesilaus II (ca. 444-360 B.C.), the Spartan king in 398 B.C., was asked why the walls had never been built. Pointing to almost the entire male population of the city, engaging in one of their frequent military drills, the king said, "These are the walls of Lacedaemon."

"Might makes right!"

"Woe to the vanquished!"

(Brennus, ca. 390 B.C.)

"Rome is accustomed to delivering herself with iron, not with gold!"

(Camillus, early 300's B.C.)

In about the year 390 B.C., the Gauls under Brennus invaded Rome and sacked most of the city. To this day it is not known whether Brennus was the Gaulic chieftan's name or his title. But at any rate, only the garrison of Rome's small inner citadel managed to hold out. This part of the fortifications would have fallen too but for the cackling of the sacred temple geese that alerted the defenders to a stealthy night-time attempt to scale the citadel's steep walls.

After about six months of occupation the Gauls became restless and agreed to leave the area upon payment of 1000 pounds of gold. The Romans managed to find the necessary precious metal in hiding places throughout the countryside. But when the gold was placed on the balance scales, a dispute arose. According to the Roman historical version, Brennus stepped into the middle of the quarrel and declared it an an end. He asserted that "might makes right!" One of the Roman leaders attempted to carry on the argument, but the protest did not last long. Brennus reportedly threw his sword onto the side of the balance alongside the weights and cried out, "Woe to the vanquished!"

Historical accounts differ as to what happened to the Gauls when they left Rome with their loot. The Greek historian Polybius reported that the Gauls returned to their homeland and lived peacefully. According to the account of the Roman historian Livy, a Roman army was quickly assembled, pursuing and defeating the departing Gauls. The leader of this Roman army, Marcus Furius Camilus (d. 365 B.C.) allegedly had the last word, declaring that "Rome is accustomed to delivering herself with iron, not with gold!"

But at any rate, the famous cry of Brennus, "Might makes right!" has echoed and re-echoed down through history, along with his second assertion, "Woe to the vanquished!"

"No city is impregnable into which an ass, laden with gold, can be led."

(Philip II, King of Macedon, ca. 340 B.C.)

Philip II (382-336 B.C.), father of Alexander the Great, was a bold and warlike ruler. He had the ability to accomplish by intrigue some of the things he could not gain by force. Ruler of the small Greek state of Macedon, Philip managed to take over the rule of all of the squabbling city states of Greece by the time he was assassinated at the age of 45.

Earlier, Philip had gone to the Greek temple at Delphi to ask whether the omens were favorable for his future. "Fight with silver spears and you will conquer everywhere," was the reply of the oracle. Philip took this to mean that bribery could be used to gain control of some of the other cities with which he was at odds.

Somewhat later, Philip said that "no city is impregnable into which an ass, laden with gold, can be led."

The early Greeks, of course, were not alone in the use of bribery for political or military objectives. About this same time in history a Roman proverb stated: "A golden key opens any gate."

"He talks of passing from Europe to Asia,
but cannot pass from one couch to another!"

(Alexander the Great, 336 B.C.)

The independent Greek city-states had long dreamed of uniting to make war in Asia against their traditional foreign enemy, the Persian Empire. Under the leadership of Philip II, the energetic, forceful king of Macedonia, these plans began to be realized.

In his personal life, Philip was estranged from his wife Olympias, a bitter woman given to mysticism and hypnotic trances. But both Philip and Olympias were quite fond of their only child, Alexander (356-323 B.C.). Tutored in classical studies by Aristotle (384-322 B.C.), Alexander had been furnished the best military training available by actual experience in his father's army.

As was often the custom of kings in those days, Philip decided to marry a more compatible woman, Cleopatra, as a second wife. At the wedding feast, Philip and most of his generals drank themselves into insensibility.

Observing his drunken father and his generals, who had bragged of their plans to invade Asia, Alexander sarcastically commented, "he talks of passing from Europe to Asia, but cannot pass from one couch to the other!"

Shortly after, Olympias abetted an associate named Pausanias to murder Philip, possibly with the knowledge of Alexander, although this is not known for certain. After the death of his father, Alexander became king and made himself master of Greece. Alexander then invaded Asia, "as he never thought of not doing it; it was his inheritance." The youthful Alexander then followed his father's plans to world conquest.

"So would I, were I Parmenio."

(Alexander the Great, 331 B.C.)

By 331 B.C. Alexander the Great's small Greek army controlled the eastern coasts of the Mediterranean. Still uncrippled by battle, Emperor Darius III of Persia (ca. 380-330 B.C.) offered to cede large areas of land west of the Euphrates river to Alexander, in exchange for Alexander's pledge to withdraw.

Parmenio, an able general, but without Alexander's vision, stated that if he were Alexander he would accept the offer of Darius.

But the audacious and brilliant Alexander quickly replied, "So would I, were I Parmenio." Not being he, Alexander went on to victory.

"More worlds to conquer."

(attributed to Alexander the Great, ca. 323 B.C.)

Alexander the Great lived only 32 years and eight months. In that brief time he grew to manhood in Greece, trained and assembled an army, inspired and led it, and made himself master of the known world. He then set out to rule lands that were even beyond the limits of geographical knowledge. Much of his military success may have been due to his willingness to fight at the head of his troops.

After Alexander's armies had subdued the armies of all the lands known to the Greeks, tradition says that Alexander begged for "more worlds to conquer."

Falling ill shortly after his military victories, Alexander was dead within a matter of a few days. Some of Alexander's generals managed to hold on to subjugated territories, ruling individual areas as king. But much of Alexander's world quickly slipped away, retaining little of Alexander's influence.

"To the best."

(Alexander the Great, 323 B.C.)

In his brief lifetime, Alexander the Great had accomplished more than any previous military man in history. From a cultural standpoint, he had lifted the civilized world out of one groove and had set it in another, exposing the whole to the knowledge and art of the Greeks. Yet it remained to be seen if he could preside over a world empire at peace.

But perhaps Alexander had dreamed a dream too great for the accomplishment of any one mortal. At any rate, he fell ill, and on the tenth day his closest companions and generals were convinced he lay dying. Alexander himself seemed to sense this, and as his officers came to pay their respects, one asked to which of his generals Alexander would leave his vast empire.

"To the best," whispered Alexander, and that evening he died.

For a time there was a movement to organize the army, with a general as a regent for Alexander's unborn child (his Persian wife, Roxane, was soon to give birth). But the common soldiers declared that as Macedonian Greeks they would never obey the son of a Persian woman.

Interminable conflicts then divided Alexander's erstwhile companions, and night now fell on his brief empire. For twenty years it was convulsed by bloody struggles, and eventually divided among his generals, none of whom was strong enough to qualify as "the best."

"Under the yoke"

(traditional, 321 B.C.)

In 321 B.C. a Roman army was decisively beaten by the Samnites, a Latin neighbor of the Romans, in an encounter at the Caudine Forks, in the southwest of Italy.

The surviving Roman troops who offered to surrender were forced to pass under a symbolic yoke of spears bound together, and then were forced into slavery.

The custom of passing under a yoke of spears may have originated at this time, or it may have already been an ancient token of disgrace long before. At any rate, the term "under the yoke" has ever since been used to designate a condition of bondage.

"Another such victory and I am lost!"

"A Pyrrhic victory."

(Pyrrhus, ca. 280 B.C.)

In about 280 B.C., Pyrrhus (319-272 B.C.), king of the small Greek kingdom of Epirus, took his army from Greece to southern Italy, to aid his allies the Tarentines against their traditional enemy, the Romans.

At the fiercely contested battle of Asculum, the troops of Pyrrhus routed the Romans, who fled the field. Assessing his own losses immediately after the battle, Pyrrhus was struck by the high percentage of casualties among his elite troops and his war elephants. "Another such victory and I am lost!" was his cry of anguish.

The expression, "a Pyrrhic victory," has come down through history to mean a hollow triumph, any victory won at too great a cost.

Pyrrhus, a second cousin of Alexander the Great, was generally regarded as an excellent commander. But after another series of battles with the Romans, who did not seem to know when they had been defeated, Pyrrhus was compelled to return to Greece.

While Pyrrhus had been absent in Italy, his enemies at home had taken over the government of his Macedonian kingdom. Nothing daunted, Pyrrhus set out to win back his throne. He had almost completed the task when he led a night attack against the city of Argos. During this assault, Pyrrhus was stunned by a tile thrown by a woman from a housetop on the city wall, and was killed by the soldiers of his enemies before he could recover his feet.

"These mountains do not touch the sky."

(Hannibal, 219 B.C.)

Rome and Carthage fought a life and death struggle — a series of wars to settle the military and trade supremacy of the Mediterranean world. It would be an over simplification to say that this great dispute was essentially a contest between the might of Rome's armies and the brilliance of one Carthaginian leader, Hannibal (247-183 B.C.), who has sometimes been called "the finest general the world has produced." Nevertheless, the famous Roman historian, Polybius, reported that "of all that befell Rome, the cause was one man."

Gathering an army in Spain, Hannibal planned to march by land to Italy, thus avoiding the Roman domination of the seas. No one had ever tried such a march before, and geographers said there was no passable route through the forbidding, snow-covered Alps. Besides, Hannibal's soldiers had heard many tales of the fierceness of the natives in that mountainous area. Of perhaps greater difficulty, his army was hampered by supply problems and by the elephants that were to be taken.

Modern scholars have long puzzled over the route that Hannibal took through the Alps. And even today historians are not in complete agreement as to the pass that he used. Regardless of the physical difficulties, perhaps Hannibal's greatest problem lay in persuading his superstitious soldiers from the lowlands to follow him into the cold, trackless mountains, the like of which none of them had ever seen.

"These mountains do not touch the sky," Hannibal reportedly told his troops from sunny Spain. And he never wavered in leading them upward through the passes between the great peaks.

Coming down on the plains of Italy, to the rear of the Romans, Hannibal defeated army after army made up of troops that were considered the best in the ancient world. For 17 years his outnumbered, dwindling army dominated all of Italy except the city of Rome itself. But he never had the manpower or engines of siege to break down the city's walls. Eventually, the Romans and their allies wore Hannibal down, causing his withdrawal and eventual defeat in Africa.

Even 200 years later, the famous Roman writer Juvenal said that Roman mothers who wanted to frighten their children had only to call out, "Hannibal's at the gates!" *("Hannibal ad portas!")*.

"Fabian tactics"

(traditional)

In 218 B.C. the Carthaginians crossed the Alps with elephants and struck at the Romans from the rear. The brilliant cavalry played havoc with the rashly-led Latins. Never before, the perhaps never again in ancient times would troops of the caliber of the Roman Legions be cut to pieces in such devastating fashion. At Rome, the government was in near panic.

As was the Roman custom in times of grave crisis, the elected Consuls agreed to step aside and turn their powers over to a dictator named by the Senate. Fabius Maximus (d. 203 B.C.), commonly known as Fabian, was given this supreme command.

Fabian realized that Hannibal had only a limited number of troops, and that he might not receive reinforcements from Carthage. Fabian also knew that the best of the Romans could not stand up to the strategies of Hannibal. Accordingly, Fabian began a "scorched earth" policy to deprive the invaders of supplies. He also adopted so-called "Fabian tactics," picking off stragglers, and setting ambushes when feasible. He avoided pitched battles and depended on the Roman farmers to bring cattle and food stuffs inside the city walls. Slowly, he ground down the strength of the Carthaginians.

There was much grumbling at Fabian, as the Romans had always believed in meeting their enemies face to face. Fabian delayed battle so long that he was called "Cunctator" (the delayer). But in the end, Fabian's tactics won out.

Hannibal won every battle that was fought, but he continued to lose strength. Given little support by his government at Carthage, Hannibal never got the equipment he needed to take the city of Rome. He was finally forced to evacuate the Carthaginian army, after 15 years without a defeat.

When the well-known Fabian Society was founded by some of the world's leading socialists in England in 1884, the organization took its name from the famous old Roman. The society's stated purpose was to bring about socialism by gradual, rather than by revolutionary means, through tactics reminiscent of Fabian.

"Let us relieve the Romans from the anxiety they have so long experienced..."

(Hannibal, 183 B.C.)

Hannibal (247-183 B.C.) was the most feared enemy that Rome ever had. He was a military genius who beat the Roman Legions in battle after battle, even though frequently outnumbered. In the Second Punic War (218-201 B.C.), Hannibal controlled most of Italy for over 15 years, excepting the city of Rome itself.

For 17 years after the Second Punic War Hannibal managed to stay out of the grasp of the Romans. He found asylum in one place after another far to the east, usually at the court of a king who had not been subdued by the Romans. Bythnia was still an independent kingdom when Roman agents traced Hannibal to that place in 183 B.C. The king of Bythnia had given his pledge that Hannibal would be safe there, but after a time the king bowed to Roman pressure.

Telling Hannibal that he must allow the Romans to take him, the king gave Hannibal a few moments in a locked room. Hannibal, of course, knew that he would be taken to Rome in a cage, paraded through the streets, and then tortured to death. To the king he said, "Let us relieve the Romans from the anxiety they have so long experienced, since it tries their patience too much to wait for an old man's death." Hannibal then took poison from a secret compartment of a ring, dying within a few minutes.

"Besides, Carthage must be destroyed!"

(Marcus Porcius Cato, 174 B.C.)

In the third century before Christ, Rome and Carthage were the two greatest military and economic powers in the world. These two great powers were involved in the so-called three Punic Wars. The first of these struggles was from 264 to 241 B.C. There was peace for a time, and fighting again broke out. The second Punic war lasted from 218 to 201 B.C. The Carthaginian general Hannibal beat the Romans in battle after battle but was finally forced to withdraw his armies from Italy when his men and supplies were not replaced. Carthage eventually surrendered.

Marcus Porcius Cato (234-149 B.C.) was an able general and good statesman who was sent by Rome to Carthage to supervise some of the terms of surrender of that power. Cato, who had a strong fear of the power of Carthage, formed the impression that Carthage had completely recovered from the effects of the Second Punic War and would again be a threat to the power of Rome.

Cato was a Roman Senator. When he returned to Rome he made many forceful speeches. He ended all of his public statements or speeches, on whatever subject, with the dour statement, "besides, Carthage must be destroyed!"

In the Third Punic War, 149-146 B.C., Rome completely destroyed Carthage, selling the survivors into slavery and tearing down the city.

"If we must fight and kill,
let us fight for ourselves."

"If you are men, follow me!"

(Spartacus, ca. 73 and 71 B.C.)

Spartacus (d. 71 B.C.), a Greek from Thrace, was a shepherd in his youth. Later, while serving as a soldier he was captured by the Romans and sold to the master of a training school for gladiators at Capua, Italy.

The life of a gladiator was, of course, one of great peril. The loser in the duels was usually killed and his body dragged unceremoniously from the arena with hooks.

There is no known record of the number of duels that Spartacus was forced to fight. But according to tradition, he told other gladiators that "if we must fight and kill, let us fight for ourselves." With about 70 other captive gladiators, Spartacus ran away and hid in the crater of Mount Vesuvius. Other slaves, who were not regularly kept in chains, then deserted the Roman estates and joined the band with Spartacus.

Civil authorities came with a large number of Roman soldiers, but they were quickly defeated by Spartacus' determined slaves. This caused a great exodus of slaves from Rome, with an estimated 100,000 flocking to join his movement.

Spartacus intended to lead his army out of Italy and then to disband it, so the freed slaves could return to their original homes. Two Roman armies pursued him into the Po River region of northern Italy, but Spartacus' well-organized followers defeated both.

In 72 B.C., believing they were masters of all of Italy, the freed slaves then demanded to be led back to Rome. Whether Spartacus himself favored this action is unknown. At any rate, the slave army turned back toward Rome in considerable dissension. Another Roman army under Marcus Licinius Crassus (115-53 B.C.) then fell upon them and managed to defeat the revolters.

Spartacus continued to win some minor engagements as he attempted to cross over into Sicily. He was betrayed, however, by boatmen who had agreed to transport the slaves. Crassus, in the meantime continued to pick off stragglers and surrounded the entire group. According to tradition, Spartacus urged his followers, "If you are men, follow me!"

Some accounts say that Spartacus was killed, fighting bitterly to the end. Other records indicate Spartacus and 6,000 other slaves were crucified and their bodies left hanging for months as a grim warning to others who might be tempted to run away.

"Caesar's wife must be above suspicion!"

(Julius Caesar, 62 B.C.)

In 62 B.C. Gaius Julius Caesar (102?-44 B.C.) one of the most able men ever to feel the "pulse of power" in ancient Rome, suspected that his wife Pompeia was carrying on an affair with one Publius Clodius. Actually, Caesar had not a shred of credible evidence, yet he proceeded to divorce her nevertheless.

Under questioning by a friend as to why he had thus divorced Pompeia, in view of the dearth of proof, Caesar was quoted by the Roman Historian Suetonius: "Because I maintain that the members of my family should be free not only from guilt, but from even the suspicion of guilt."

Hundreds of years later, Shakespeare distilled the explanation to read, "Caesar's wife must be above suspicion."

"I have crossed the Rubicon."

(Julius Caesar, 49 B.C.)

Gaius Julius Caesar (102?-44 B.C.), one of the most able men produced in the Roman world, was outstanding alike as a general, statesman, and writer. The founder of the Roman Empire, he was also the destroyer of republican liberties. To many, he was the champion of the common people, but to others Caesar was nothing short of a demagogue.

Toward the end of 61 B.C., Caesar formed a political alliance with the victorious Roman general Pompey (106-48 B.C.) and with Crassus (115-53 B.C.), a man of almost unlimited wealth. As a politician, Caesar's popularity enabled him to be assigned as military governor of Gaul and other provinces. In the eight years from 58 to 51 B.C., Caesar proved himself as a military commander, subduing army after army of barbarians, and organizing the government of the new territory.

At Rome, affairs were turning against Caesar. Crassus died, and Caesar's military triumphs in Gaul made Pompey so jealous that Pompey persuaded the Roman Senate to order Caesar to lay down his arms or be declared an enemy of the state.

Faced with the choice of returning to the life of a private citizen or going back to Italy to contend with Pompey for domination of the Roman world, Caesar responded by leading his single legion across the Rubicon, the small stream that then marked the border between Gaul and Italy. As a stream, the Rubicon was insignificant, but once Caesar's legions waded across it, there could be no turning back, and that is the meaning that has come down through the years.

Caesar went ahead to defeat Pompey and become master of the Roman world. He was eventually murdered in 44 B.C. by those who believed he had made himself a Roman emperor in fact, if not in name.

"Thumbs down!"

"Hail Emperor! We who are about to die salute you!"

(traditional, Roman gladiators)

The Romans long had gladiatorial bouts in arenas and later in colosseums, the most notable of which was at Rome itself. Often the shouting and din of the crowd was nearly unbearable when one of these bouts was in progress. At times it was customary for the Emperor or official presiding at the games to decide the fate of a combatant who had fallen to the ground or received a crippling wound. If the fallen one had fought with skill and courage, the Emperor would often signal "thumbs up" as a request that the unfortunate gladiator be spared. If the signal was "thumbs down" it meant the winning gladiator was immediately to dispatch the fallen.

After a time it became the custom to march in all gladiators in a sort of parade at the beginning of the gladiatorial games. Some of these were professional gladiators who fought for acclaim or for a fee, but others in the procession were often slaves, criminals, or war captives, condemned to fight until death. By tradition, when the parade ended, the fighters stood in a line facing the Emperor's box. Then the gladiators recited the mournful, prophetic chant: "Hail Emperor! We who are about to die salute you!"

"Beware the Ides of March."

"You too, Brutus?"
«Et tu, Brute?»

(latter phrase attributed to Julius Caesar, 44 B.C.)

A Roman of great ability, Gaius Julius Caesar (102?-44 B.C.) was outstanding as a military general, a statesman, a writer, and a politician. Perhaps as clearly as any man of his time, Caesar realized that the Roman Senate was no longer capable of solving the complex problems that faced a vast empire. Caesar's solution was to place all power into the hands of one man — himself.

There was not much question that Caesar was a single-minded dictator. But Caesar used much of his power to bring about important reforms for the public welfare. Knowing the Roman people's hatred of kings, Caesar had refused the crown, but he was dictator nonetheless.

Some men believed that the Roman Republic could be restored by eliminating Caesar, so a plot to murder him resulted. Caesar's old political ally and former friend Brutus joined in the plan. On March 15, 44 B.C. (the Ides of March), after being warned (according to Shakespeare) by a soothsayer to "Beware the Ides of March," Caesar went anyway to the Senate that day but on the steps there he received many stab wounds from men in high places who had accepted his favors and that he considered friends. "You too, Brutus?" (or, "Even you, Brutus?"), asked Caesar as the daggers struck home ("Et tu, Brute?" Shakespeare has him say, in Latin).

Apparently Caesar had misjudged his relationships with a number of people. Some said that Caesar had provoked his own fate, as much by the ostentatiousness of his rule as by the exercise of power itself.

"I came, I saw, I conquered."
« *Veni, vidi, vici.* »

(Julius Caesar, 47 B.C.)

A magnificent procession called a "triumph" was the highest honor that could be given to a victorious general by the Roman Senate. Those fortunate enough to receive this honor entered the city in a magnificent carriage drawn by four horses. The Senators themselves walked at the head of the procession, while a public holiday was declared. After the Senators came trumpeters, wagons bearing spoils of war, and important prisoners such as defeated generals and kings, who were dragged along in chains.

The triumphant general carried a scepter and wore a wreath of olive leaves, while a slave held a golden crown high above the victor's head. Coming close behind were the troops, carrying spoils they had been awarded, singing songs of praise to the Roman gods and to their general.

After a time some of the more vainglorious generals who were awarded triumphs began to exhibit scale models on wagons, showing fortified cities they had captured. At other times, graphic portrails of the military campaign were carried, to enhance the reputation of the general involved.

In 47 B.C. Julius Caesar was voted a triumph following his subjugation of King Pharnaces II of Pontus. Not wanting to appear overly vain, Caesar ignored the usual displays of spoils and showpieces. Instead, Caesar confined most of his display to signs intended to show the speed and efficiency with which he had won the victory. With laconic simplicity, his signs read, *"Veni, vidi, vici"* (Latin for "I came, I saw, I conquered").

"If the nose of Cleopatra had been shorter,
the whole face of the earth would have been changed."

(Blaise Pascal, 1600's)

Some of the "ifs" in history may be argued endlessly. For example, the Egyptian Princess Cleopatra (69-30 B.C.) obviously had

144 □ Famous Phrases

great influence over Marc Antony (ca. 82-30 B.C.), the young Roman who emerged as perhaps the single most powerful figure in the world after the assassination of Julius Caesar.

Instead of rallying his legions to meet Octavian (63 B.C.-A.D. 41) in battle, Marc Antony seemed unable to pull himself away from the beautiful Egyptian Princess. When Antony did finally get around to leading his legions to battle against Octavian at the battle of Actium (31 B.C.), his chances had diminished greatly. Antony's legions were well aware that he did not want to fight. Octavian, however made the most of his opportunities, and defeated Antony.

Contemplating what might have happened if Antony had not been so distracted by Cleopatra, the French writer and philosopher Blaise Pascal (1623-1662), wrote: "If the nose of Cleopatra had been shorter [i.e., had she been less beautiful], the whole face of the earth would have been changed."

"All roads lead to Rome."

(attributed to Augustus, ca. 20's B.C.)

The skill of Roman engineers and the availability of slave labor made Roman roads the finest the world had ever known until recent times. The earliest roads in Italy and in the provinces were originally built for military purposes—to facilitate the moving of supplies and troops as they might be needed. But after a short time it was clear to almost every Roman that good roads encouraged commerce and travel.

Beginning with the route called the Appian Way, built in 312 B.C., the construction of highways kept pace with the expansion of Roman boundaries. At the height of the Empire, there was a great network, with Rome as the hub, of approximately 50,000 miles of roadway.

Close by the edifice called the Rostra in Rome was the so-called "Golden Milestone," on which the Emperor Augustus (63 B.C.-A.D. 14) had enscribed the names of all the great routes converging there, with the distances to the chief cities along their way. Some say the inscription proclaimed that "all roads lead to Rome."

Whatever the legend on the inscription, it was certain that all roads—governmental, cultural, industrial, military, or those involving trade and art—indeed centered in Rome.

"I found Rome of clay;
I leave it to you of marble."

"Have I played well the part?"

(Augustus, ca. A.D. 10)

The young Roman named Gaius Octavius, grandnephew and adopted son of Julius Caesar, plunged the Roman Republic into civil war after Caesar was assassinated by political enemies. In the struggle that followed, Octavian triumphed over his opponents and assumed power in 27 B.C. under the title of "Augustus" ("exalted one"). He thus became first emperor in name of the Roman world.

After some border wars, Augustus brought about the longest period of peace the ancient world had ever seen. With the Romans free of war, he promoted marriage and regulated divorce, built roads, improved living conditions, revived agriculture, encouraged industry, and abolished some of the abuses of government. He also established the first police and fire departments in Rome and adorned the capital city. Although there were always some who regarded him as a tyrant, for controlling elections arbitrarily and imposing censorship, for example, Augustus accomplished much.

The Roman historian Dio wrote that in the emperor's later years he bragged, "I found Rome of clay [brick]. I leave it to you [posterity] of marble."

As he approached the end of his life, Augustus was apparently serene and in good spirits. As his strength slowly ebbed, he called one day for a mirror. Arranging his hair, he asked those present, "Have I played well the part [of Emperor]?"

When his officials had assured Augustus that he had used his power with restraint and wisdom, the Emperor repeated the lines of a classical Greek drama that was popular at the time, "Then clap your hands and take me off the stage."

"Let him murder his mother, but be emperor."

(Agrippina, A.D. 37)

Agrippina (ca. A.D. 15-59), mother of Nero (A.D. 37-68) visited a fortuneteller while pregnant who told her she was carrying a child who would become the Roman Emperor. The fortuneteller also predicted that the child would eventually kill Agrippina.

Ambitious to be the mother of an Emperor, Agrippina reportedly blurted out, "Let him murder his mother, but be emperor."

Agrippina realized her ambition, but unfortunately the predictions of the fortuneteller were true, and in A.D. 59 Nero had her killed.

"Would that the Romans had but one neck!"

(Caligula, A.D. 39)

"The king can do no wrong!"

(William Blackstone, 1769)

"The divine right of kings."

(traditional)

"Power corrupts; absolute power corrupts absolutely."

(Lord John Acton)

Historical literature is full of accounts of rulers who considered themselves above the control of any human agency. The ancient Roman writer told the Roman Emperor Trajan (A.D. 52/3 to 117) that "the gods have given you supreme power and control over all things, even over yourself."

Another Roman writer, Suetonius, said that when the grandmother of the infamous Emperor Caligula tried to advise him,

Caligula retorted, "Remember that I have the right to do anything to anybody!"

In the exercise of the right which Caligula believed accrued to all monarchs, he was embarrassed by the large number of his subjects. When for instance the crowd at the amphitheater cheered the gladiator Caligula wanted to lose, the Emperor exclaimed in frustrated anger, "Would that the people of Rome had but one neck!" According to historical records, Caligula often said, "Let them hate me, so they but fear me!"

European rulers during and after the Middle Ages, especially the kings in England, France, and Germany, maintained that the monarch was the immediate earthly representative of the deity. The famous English legal writer, Blackstone, went so far as to say in his *Commentaries* (1769) that "The king can do no wrong!"

The English civil war begun in 1642 and the French revolution begun in 1789 finally came about in dispute by the people of the doctrine of divine right. In Germany, even as late as the time of William II (1859-1941) that monarch frequently contended in his speeches that he was ruler by divine right.

Whatever the source of a king's power, the British historian, Lord Acton (1834-1902) commented that "Power corrupts; absolute power corrupts absolutely."

"Nero fiddled while Rome burned."

(traditional)

"What an artist dies in me!"

(Nero, A.D. 64)

Emperor of Rome for 14 years (A.D. 54-68), Nero Claudius Caesar Drusus Germanicus (A.D. 37-68) was usually known simply as Nero. Celebrated for his depravity, he murdered his tutor, the famous philosopher Seneca (ca. 4 B.C.-A.D. 65), his mother, his wife, and his mistress, along with many lesser individuals.

Nero made no secret of the fact that he considered himself one of the most talented singers, poets, and musical performers that had ever lived. He traveled in luxury throughout Italy and Greece, granting special privileges to the Greeks because they loudly applauded his musical performances.

In A.D. 64 fire of unknown origin broke out in Rome. The city was one of the largest and most densely populated in the world; many of the buildings were then constructed of wood. The flames raged out of control for six days, abated somewhat, and then broke out anew. Losses in lives and property were catastrophic. A few days later, plague swept through the ruined areas. Some of the superstitious people in the streets blamed the tragedy on the wrath of the gods, but others spread the rumor that Nero had set the blaze. This story spread almost as quickly as the flames, as Nero was believed capable of any evil and there was considerable unrest in every level of society.

Realizing this rumor could undermine the little support he still had among his subjects, Nero is believed to have diverted attention from himself by persecuting Christians. Nevertheless, the story persisted that Nero was playing his lyre and singing during the fire, without the slightest concern for his fellow Romans. Eventually, the masses became so tired of Nero's excesses that a revolt broke out. Realizing what was happening, Nero attempted to escape. He committed suicide as his pursuers came near.

The violin was probably unknown until about 1600, but the saying persists that "Nero fiddled while Rome burned." It is more likely that he was playing on a lyre or a lute.

Vain performer to the end, Nero lamented bitterly as he committed suicide, "What an artist dies in me!"

*"No matter how many you slay,
you cannot kill your successor."*

(Seneca, A.D. 59)

The famous Roman philosopher was the tutor of Nero for a time in Nero's youth. Seneca (ca. 4 B.C.-A.D. 65) took Nero to task for needlessly killing so many people who had only mildly displeased the emperor. "No matter how many you slay, you cannot kill your successor," said Seneca, whom Nero turned on shortly and killed also.

"Bread and circuses"

(Juvenal, ca. A.D. 98)

The Roman writer Juvenal (A.D. 60?-140?) furnished us considerable insight into daily life in Rome. Juvenal said that the moral fiber of the average citizen had deteriorated until people were more interested in free bread rations, free gladiatorial fights, and free circuses than in earning their own way.

Juvenal may have exaggerated somewhat. But there is good reason to believe the Roman emperors after Trajan thought they could buy the support of the common people. The idea apparently was that almost anything would be overlooked if the emperor showered handouts on the citizens of Rome.

Juvenal's theme of "bread and circuses" has been repeated in a number of different periods of history.

"He who lives by the sword shall perish by the sword."

(paraphrased from Matthew 26:52)

"It is easier to commit than to justify a parricide."

(Papinian, A.D. 212)

"Uneasy lies the head that wears a crown."

(Shakespeare's *Henry IV*)

The Roman Emperor Septimius Severus (A.D. 146-211) left his throne jointly to his two sons, Caracalla (ca. A.D. 188-217) and Geta

(d. 212). Even before Severus' death, Caracalla had revealed his complete lack of character by trying to induce Roman troops to murder his father.

As joint emperors, the two sons quickly divided the Roman world into rival camps. Each of the brothers went to great pains to stay under the protection of their respective armed guard. Julia, mother of the two emperors, worked out a plan for splitting the empire in two parts, giving the younger brother Geta the area in the east. At a conference to straighten out details of the division, Caracalla managed to secrete some of his soldiers behind a curtain in his mother's apartment. Caracalla's troops then killed Geta even while Julia tried to shield him from the assassins with her own body.

Completely ruthless, Caracalla then had approximately 20,000 Romans killed because they had been partisans of Geta. Caracalla also forced his mother to withhold any visible sign of grief on pain of instant death.

Realizing that he had caused terrible unrest among his subjects in Rome, Caracalla turned to Papinian (A.D. 146?-212) for help. Papinian was the statesman and eminent lawyer who had been first minister of the government under Septimius Severus. Caracalla ordered Papinian to use his prestige and oratorical ability to justify the murder of Geta to the Roman public.

But Papinian would not compromise his principles. "It is easier to commit than to justify a parricide [murder of close kin]," he told Caracalla, signing his own death warrant by his refusal.

In his own turn, Caracalla was assassinated five years later. The Roman Senate, without a dissenting vote, passed a resolution to "brand Caracalla with eternal infamy."

History can point to scores of examples to prove the timeless Biblical truth; Jesus said (in Matthew 26:52), "all they that take the sword shall perish with the sword." This is commonly paraphrased as above.

Hundreds of years after the time of the bloody emperor Caracalla, Shakespeare wrote his famous line, "Uneasy lies the head that wears a crown." Shakespeare was describing events in the perilous reign of the English King Henry IV (1366-1413), but was writing not only for that time but for all ages.

"When in Rome, do as the Romans do"

(St. Ambrose, A.D. 300's)

St. Ambrose (339-397), one of the leaders in the early church, wrote a letter of advice to St. Augustine. In this communication St. Ambrose said: "If you are at Rome, live in the Roman style. If you are elsewhere, live as they live elsewhere."

"There, where I have passed,
the grass will never grow again."

"Scourge of God"

(Attila the Hun, ca. 451)

During the A.D. 300's and 400's a vast army of Mongolian nomads called the Huns swept across Europe, plundering and looting with impunity. The tribes' warriors lived on horseback, their women in carts; they were tough, daring raiders, skilled bowmen, and adept at hit-and-run warfare.

Only the famous walls of Constantinople saved the great capitol of the Eastern Roman Empire in 450 from the invaders, who dressed in animal skins or coarse cloth and were described as the most repulsive warriors that ever lived. Proud of the scorched earth his horde left behind, "There where I have passed the grass will never grow again," bragged their leader, Attila.

The next year it became Western Europe's turn to tremble at the invasion, whose leader described himself as "Attila the Hun, the Scourge of God." It seemed Attila might sweep all of Christendom before him, leading his host of Huns, Alani, and barbaric German tribes deep into Gaul (modern France).

Somewhere near Chalons (now France) in June, 451, the Roman armies of Aetius joined forces with the army of Theodoric, the King of the Visigoths who inhabited much of Gaul. These combined armies met the Huns in one of the most important and bloodiest encounters in ancient times. While the battle was not a complete victory for either side, Attila was forced to retreat and his power was broken. He died two years later and the Huns' threat to the civilization of Europe quickly melted away.

The people of Europe never forgot the devastating ravages, the vandalism, or the fearsome appearance of the Huns. Hundreds of years after the time of Attila, the French people commonly used the name "Huns" as a term of contempt for the Germans in World War I (1914-18).

Index

A

Achilles 121
"Achilles heel" 121
Acton, John, *Lord* 147
Adams, Abigail 10
Adams, John 14
Adams, Samuel 5
"After me, the deluge!" 87
Age of Pericles 128, 129
Agelisaus of Sparta 130
"ages| Now he belongs to the" 42
Agrippina 147
"aircraft carrier. Am trailing same.|
  Sighted" 60
Alexander the Great 132, 133
Alfred (U.S. ship) 11
"all hang together, or assuredly we
  shall all hang separately!| We
  must" 12
"All men are created equal" 13
"All roads lead to Rome" 145
Allen, Ethan 9
Allen, William 29
"alliances| Steer clear of permanent"
  19
"Along this track of pathless ocean
  it is my intention to steer" 74
"altereth not| The law of the Medes
  and Persians, that" 124
Ambrose, *Saint* 152
"American Continents ... are hence-
  forth not to be considered as sub-
jects for future colonization by
  any European powers" 24
American Crisis (pamphlet) 15
"The American War is over, but this
  is far from being the case with the
  American Revolution" 16
"ammunition| Praise the Lord and
  pass the" 64
"Another such victory and I am
  lost" 135
Antoinette, Marie *(Queen of France)*
  90, 93
"Any weapon that kills—large or
  small—is evil in the hands of a
  killer" 65
Appian Way 145
"Après moi, le deluge!" 87
Arc, Joan of (Jeanne d'Arc) 73
Aristotle 132
"An army, like a serpent, travels on
  its belly" 87
"An army travels on its stomach" 87
Arouet, François Marie (real name
  of Voltaire) 89
"...arsenal of democracy" 56
"artist dies in me!| What an" 148
"Ask not what your country can do
  for you; ask what you can do for
  your country" 68
"an ass, laden with gold" 131
"atheists in fox holes| There are no"
  64
atomic bomb 87

"attack!| My left yields; my right is broken through; ... I" 107

"attack!| The best means of defense is to" 107

Attila the Hun 152

Augustus (Caesar Augustus, real name Octavian) 145, 146

B

"bad peace| There never was a good war or a" 6

"balance of power" 77

Barnum, Phineas Taylor (P.T.) 34

Barron, James 23

Bartholdi, Fredric 33

"battalions| God is on the side of the heavy" 99

"The Battle of Waterloo was won on the playing fields of Eaton" 99

"The battle, sir, is not to the strong alone..." 7

"bayonet!| Go tell your master ... that we will leave here only at the point of a" 90

"Be easy with him, boys!" 50

"Be of good cheer, the water is coming" 79

Beauregard, P.G.T. 36

Bee, Bernard E. 37

Bell, Alexander Graham 46

"belly| An army, like a serpent, travels on its" 87

Belshazzar 123

Bennington, battle of 17

"Besides, Carthage must be destroyed!" 138

"best| To the" 133

"The best means of defense is to attack!" 107

"Beware of Greeks bearing gifts" 121, 122

"Beware the Ides of March" 143

"big stick| Speak softly and carry a" 51

"bird in a cage| Only my father could keep such a" 82

"bitter water, the king lays on thee this punishment| Thou" 126

Blackstone, William 147

"Blitzkrieg" 109

"block busters" 61

"blood and iron!| Questions of the day are not decided by speeches ... but by" 104

"Blood is thicker than water!" 32

"blood of patriots| The tree of liberty must be refreshed from time to time with the" 16

"blood, toil, tears, and sweat" 111

Bonhomme Richard (American ship) 18

Booth, John Wilkes 42

Bosquet, Pierre 104

Boston Massacre 5

"the Boy" 54

"Boys, elevate them guns a little lower!" 23

Braddock, Edward 3

Bradford, William 3

"Brazenmouth Barnum" 34

"Bread and circuses" 150

"Bread, land, and peace" 106

"breath and they are scattered| God sent forth his" 81

Breed's Hill 10, 12

Brennus 130

"British Empire| I have not become the King's First Minister to preside over the liquidation of the" 116

"British Empire| The sun never sets on the" 95

Brown v. Board of Education of Topeka 48

Brutus 143

Bryan, William Jennings 48

"The buck stops here" 65

"built in a day| Rome was not" 122

"Bull Moose" 51

Bull Run, battle of 36, 37

Bunker Hill 10, 12

"burn their houses to prevent us from sleeping in them...| A people who" 100
Burnside, Ambrose 39
"Bury contention with the war" 43
"bury you!| We will" 117
"By heaven that ship is ours!" 21
Byron, George Gordon, *Lord* 123

C

Caesar (Gaius Julius) 140, 141, 143, 144
"Caesar had his brutus; Charles the First, his Cromwell; and George the Third ... may profit by their example" 7
"cake!| Let them eat" 90
Calhoun, John C. 26, 30
Caligula 147, 148
Camillus 130
"Canossa| To go to" 71
Caracalla 150
"Carthage must be destroyed" 138
Carver, George Washington 68
"Castillian| Choose, each man, what best becomes a brave" 76
Cato (the Elder) 138
"cemetery| I don't want to rule over a" 82
Central Pacific Railroad president 44
"chains| Man is born free, but everywhere he is in" 89
"chains| The workers have nothing to lose but their" 103
Chamberlain, Neville 108
"charge of the light brigade" 103
"charity for all| With malice toward none; with" 41
Charles I *(King of England)* 83-85
Charlestown Committee of Safety 8
Chateaubriand, Celeste 102
Chesapeake (U.S. ship) 21
"a chicken in his pot" 82

"The children can't go without me — I can't leave the King, and of course the King won't go" 114
"Choose, each man, what best becomes a brave Castillian" 76
Churchill, Winston 84, 111-117
"circuses| Bread and" 150
"city is impregnable into which an ass, laden with gold, can be led| No" 131
"civilization| A woman's place in society marks the level of" 30
Clay, Henry 25, 31
Cleopatra 144-145
Collins, John Warren 33
Colón, Cristóbal 74
"color-blind| Our Constitution is" 47
Columbus, Christopher 74
"Come back with your shield — or on it" 124
Common Sense (pamphlet) 13, 15
Conant, *Colonel* 8
"conquer| More worlds to" 133
"conquer!| Rejoice, we" 125
"conquered| I came, I saw, I" 144
Constitution (U.S. ship) 21
"Constitution is color-blind| Our" 47
Continental Congress 6, 11
Cook, James 88
Cooke, Philip St. George 37
Corday, Charlotte 94
"Cotton is king!" 34
"country can do for you...| Ask not what your" 68
"...country, right or wrong!" 23
Crassus, Marcus Licinius 140
"criminals need not be judged| The greatest of all" 92
"crimes are committed in thy name!| Oh, Liberty, what" 93
Cromwell, Oliver 84
"cross of gold| You shall not crucify mankind upon a" 48
"crossed the Rubicon| I have" 141

G

Gage, *General* Thomas 8

Garfield, James A. 44

"Genius is 2% inspiration and 98% perspiration" 52

"Gentlemen may cry peace! peace! — but there is no peace! The war is actually begun" 7

George III *(King of England)* 5, 6, 7, 12

Geta 150

"Give me liberty or give me death!" 7

"Give me your tired, your poor, your huddled masses yearning to breath free" 33

gladiators 142

"Go forward, always forward!" 61

"Go stranger, and to Sparta tell that here, obeying her behests, we fell" 127

"Go tell your master ... that we will leave here only at the point of a bayonet!" 90

"Go west, young man, and grow up with the country" 31

"God| Rebellion to tyrants is obedience to'" 84

"God has been over me| The finger of" 98

"God has numbered the days of your kingdom and brought it to an end" 123

"God is on the side of the heavy battalions" 99

"God plays dice with the cosmos| I cannot believe that" 65

"God reigns and the government at Washington still lives" 44

"God sent forth his breath and they are scattered" 81

"God wrought?| What hath" 29

"gold!| Rome is accustomed to delivering herself with iron, not with" 130

"gold, can be led| No city is impregnable into which an ass, laden with" 131

"A golden key opens any gate" 131

"Good! Then we shall fight in the shade!" 127

"good war or a bad peace| There never was a" 6

"government at Washington still lives| God reigns and the" 44

Grady, Henry 35

Grant, Ulysses S. 39-40

"grass will never grow again| There, where I have passed, the" 152

"Great Compromiser" 31

"the great ones eat up the smaller ones" 128

"The greatest of all criminals need not be judged" 92

"Greeks bearing gifts| Beware of" 121

Greely, Horace 31

Green Mountain Boys 9

Gregory VII *(Pope)* 71

Grey, Sir Edward 105

"Gridley| You may fire when ready," 49

"The ground's your own!" 10

H

"Hail Emperor! We who are about to die salute you!" 142

Hale, Nathan 14

Halleck, H.W. 39

Hamilcar Barca 110

"The handwriting on the wall" 123

"hang together, or assuredly we shall all hang separately!| We must all" 12

Hannibal 135, 136, 138

"Hannibal's at the gates!" 136

Harper, Robert Goodloe 19

Harrison, William Henry 28

"Have I played well the part?" 146

J

Jackson, Andrew 23, 26-28
Jackson, Thomas Nathan ("Stonewall") 36, 37, 40
"jaws of death" 104
Jeanne d'Arc 73
Jefferson, Thomas 12, 13, 14, 16, 20, 84
Joan of Arc 73
Jones, John Paul 18
"jumbo" 34
"justice and hated iniquity...| I have loved" 71
Juvenal 136, 150

K

Kennedy, John F. 68, 111-112
Khrushchev, Nikita 117
"kill your successor| No matter how many you slay, you cannot" 149
"Kilroy was here" 64
King, Martin Luther, Jr. 68
"The king can do no wrong!" 147
"king lays on thee this punishment| Thou bitter water, the" 126
"King of Spain!| I singed the beard of the" 80
"King won't go| The children ... and I can't leave the King, and of course the" 114
"kings| The divine right of" 147
"King's First Minister to preside over the liquidation of the British Empire| I have not become the" 116
Knowlton, Thomas 14

L

"Lacedaemon| These are the walls of" 129
"Lafayette, we are here" 53

"lamp by which my feet are guided| I have but one" 6
"The lamps are going out all over Europe" 105
"land, and peace| Bread," 106
"A larger soul has seldom dwelt in house of clay" 85
"The last rail is laid, the last spike driven" 44
"launched a thousand ships| The face that" 121
"The law of the Medes and Persians, that altereth not" 124
Lawrence, *Capt.* James 21-22
Lazarus, Emma 33
Lee, Henry 20
Lee, Richard Henry 12
Lee, Robert E. 39, 40, 43
"left yields; my right is broken through; ... I attack!| My" 107
"Let him murder his mother, but be emperor" 147
"Let them eat cake!" 90
"Let them hate me, so they but fear me!" 148
"Let us relieve the Romans from the anxiety they have so long experienced" 138
Lewis and Clark Expedition 20
Lewis, *Capt.* Meriwether 20
Lewis, Robert 63
Lexington, Mass. 8
"liberty| Eternal vigilance is the price of" 95
"Liberty and Union, now and forever, one and inseparable" 25
"liberty-loving people everywhere march with you!| The hopes and prayers of" 61
"liberty or give me death!| Give me" 7
"Liberty, what crimes are committed in thy name!| Oh" 93
"light brigade" 103
"Lightning war" 109
Lincoln, Abraham 35, 36, 38-39, 41-43, 44

N

Nabodinus 123

Napoleon 87, 99, 100, 101

"nature defeated me| I defeated man, but" 100

Nelson, Horatio 96, 97

Nero 147, 148

"Nero fiddled while Rome burned" 147

"Never in the field of human conflict was so much owed by so many to so few" 112

"New Deal" 55

Newton, Isaac 86

"next of kin.| Sighted aircraft carrier.... Notify" 60

"No city is impregnable into which an ass, laden with gold, can be led" 131

"No matter how long it takes to overcome this premeditated invasion, the American people ... will win through to absolute victory!" 57

"No matter how many you slay, you cannot kill your successor" 149

"nose of Cleopatra had been shorter...| If the" 145

"not one cent for tribute!| Millions for defense—" 19

"Nothing succeeds like success" 33

"Now he belongs to the ages" 42

"Nuts!" 62

O

"ocean| This little rivulet yields its distant tribute to the parent" 20

"ocean it is my intention to steer| Along this track of pathless" 74

Octavian (Caesar Augustus) 145

"Of all that befell Rome, the cause was one man" 136

"Old Glory" 25

"The old guard dies, but never surrenders" 98

"Old Ironsides" 21

Old North Church 8

"Old Put" 9

"Old soldiers never die, they just fade away" 66

"On to Richmond!" 36

"One falls, and another falls.... Death does its work ... but the nation is immortal" 44

"one if by land, and two if by sea" 8

"one lamp by which my feet are guided| I have but" 6

"one life to lose for my country| I only regret that I have but" 14

"One World" 56

"The only good Indian is a dead Indian" 35

"The only limit to the realization of tomorrow will be our doubts of today" 63

"Only my father could keep such a bird in a cage" 82

"The only thing we have to fear is fear itself" 55

"open our city to the world| We throw" 129

"opiate of the people| Religion is the" 102

Oregon Purchase 29

Otis, James 5

"Our Constitution is color-blind, and neither knows nor tolerates classes among citizens" 47

"Our country, may she always be in the right; but our country, right or wrong!" 23

"Our Union, it must be preserved!" 26

P

Packenham, *Lord* 23

Paine, Thomas 13, 15

"Rejoice, we conquer!" 125

"Religion is the opiate of the people" 102

"Remember I have the right to do anything to anybody" 148

"Remember Pearl Harbor 57

"Remember the Maine! To hell with Spain!" 49

"rendezvous with destiny" 55

"reserves| Fortune is on the side of the last" 99

"Resolved to die free men, rather than to live as slaves" 11

"return| I shall" 58

Revere, Paul 8

"revolution, the difficulty is ... to hold it in check!| When you undertake to run a" 91

"Richmond!| On to" 36

"right| Might makes" 130

"right is broken through; ... I attack!| My left yields; my" 107

"right to say it| I do not agree with what you say, but I will defend to the death your" 89

Riqueti, Honoré Gabriel Victor 90-91

"roads lead to Rome| All" 145

Robespierre, Maximilien François de 92

Rogers' Rangers 16

Roland, Jeanne Manon Phlipon 93

"Romans from the anxiety...| Let us relieve the" 138

"Romans had but one neck!| Would that the" 147

"Rome| All roads lead to" 145

"Rome burned| Nero fiddled while" 148

"Rome, do as the Romans do| When in" 152

"Rome is accustomed to delivering herself with iron, not with gold!" 130

"Rome of clay; I leave it to you of marble| I found" 146

"Rome was not built in a day" 122

Romulus and Remus 122

Roosevelt, Eleanor 67

Roosevelt, Franklin D. 11, 55, 56, 57, 58, 63

Roosevelt, Theodore 51

Rousseau, Jean Jacques 89

"Rubicon| I have crossed the" 141

Rush, Benjamin 16

"Russians every time, but that doesn't get me anywhere| I beat the" 100

S

Schliemann, Heinrich 121

Scott, Robert Falcon 105

"Scourge of God" 152

"Scratch one flattop!" 59

Second Continental Congress 11

"sea dogs" 80

Seneca 148, 149

"separate but equal" concept 48

Serapis (British, then U.S. ship) 18

"serpent, travels on its belly| An army, like a" 87

Severus (Roman emperor) 150

Shakespeare 150

Sherman, Roger 14

Sherman, William T. 47

"shield—or on it| Come back with your" 124

"ship!| Don't give up the" 21

"ship is ours!| By heaven that" 21

"Shoot if you must, this old gray head, but spare your country's flag!" 40

"shoulders of giants| If I have seen further, it is by standing on the" 86

"Sic semper tyrannis!" 42

"Sighted aircraft carrier. Am trailing same. Please notify next of kin" 60

"Sighted sub—sank same" 58

V

Valley Forge 15, 17
Van Buren, Martin 28
Vandiver, Willard Duncan 50
"veni, vidi, vici" 144
"victor belongs the spoils| To the"
26
"victory!| Westminster Abbey or"
96
"victory and I am lost!| Another
such" 135
"Victory—victory at all costs, victory in spite of all terror, victory
however hard and long the road
may be" 111
"vigilance is the price of liberty|
Eternal" 95
Voltaire 89

W

"wall| The handwriting on the" 123
"the walls have ears" 108
"walls of the kingdom| The wooden
walls are the best" 83
"war| Bury contention with the" 43
"War is cruelty, but you cannot refine it!" 47
"War is hell!" 47
"war is one of the most effectual
means of preserving peace| To be
prepared for" 18
"...war, let it begin here!" 8
Warren, Joseph 10
"warts and all" 84
Washington, Booker T. 68
Washington, George 3, 14, 17, 18,
19, 20
"water!| Blood is thicker than" 32
"water is coming| Be of good cheer,
the" 79
Waterloo 98
"Watson, come here, I want you"
46

"We beat them today, or Mollie
Stark's a widow!" 16
"We have met the enemy and they
are ours!" 22
"We must all hang together, or as-
suredly we shall hang separately!"
12
"We shall fight on the beaches, we
shall fight on the landing grounds,
we shall fight..." 113
"We throw open our city to the
world" 129
"We will bury you!" 117
"We will leave here only at the point
of a bayonet!" 90
Webster, Daniel 10, 25, 30
"weighed in the balance and found
wanting| You have been" 123
Wellington, Arthur Wellsley (Duke
of Wellington) 98, 99
West young man| Go" 31
"Westminster Abbey or victory!" 96
"What an artist dies in me!" 148
"What hath God wrought?" 29
"what have we done?| My God," 63
"What is history, but a fable agreed
upon?" 101
"When in Rome, do as the Romans
do" 152
"When in the course of human
events, it becomes necessary for
one people to dissolve the political bands..." 13
"When you undertake to run a revo-
lution, the difficulty is not to
make it go; it is to hold it in
check" 91
"White House| from log cabin to"
32
"whites of their eyes| Don't fire until
you see the" 9
Whittier, John Greenleaf 40
"Who would have thought it?" 3
"wife must be above suspicion!|
Caesar's" 140
William of Orange 79